Five miles from Bunkum

by Spike Mays

REUBEN'S CORNER
FALL OUT THE OFFICERS
NO MORE SOLDIERING FOR ME

CHRISTOPHER KETTERIDGE
AND SPIKE MAYS

Five miles from Bunkum

A VILLAGE AND ITS CRAFTS

COUNTRY BOOK CLUB
Newton Abbot 1973

Contents

List of Quotations

Illustrations

lived here (right), next door to Reuben Ford (*from a water-colour by Christopher Ketteridge*)

6b Walton's Park in 1908

 c Bragg's Mill in working order (1910) (*photo Willie Smith, Ashdon*)

7a Ashdon Fire Brigade in force at the Flower Show: Downham, Frost, Bob Matthews and Jim Freeman, being inspected by Major Pelly and Capt. Revill (1910) (*photo Willie Smith, Ashdon; lent by Brig. T. F. J. Collins*)

 b Opening the Rifle Club (1910): Mrs Thelwell, wife of Dr Thelwell of Saffron Walden, about to fire the opening shot, attended by Squire Pelly and the population of Ashdon (*photo Willie Smith, Ashdon*)

 c Capt. Collins's beaters assembled at Bendysh Hall, Radwinter (about 1910): centre, with beard and game bag, Harry Freeman ('Jersey'); and far right, his elder son Jim Freeman, who went down in his ship the *Good Hope* during the 1914–18 war (*photo Willie Smith, Ashdon; lent by Brig. T. F. J. Collins*)

8a Wheelwright's yard (*from a water colour by Christopher Ketteridge*)

 b The old forge (*from a water-colour by Christopher Ketteridge*)

9a 'The Clayes', which the Ketteridges practically rebuilt in 1929, adding another wing which cannot be seen here. One of the examples of their work in the village

 b Arthur Grewes of Little Sampford, shepherd (1910)

10a Joslin standing on his head when the agricultural strike was over (1914)

Illustrations

LINE DRAWINGS
by Christopher Ketteridge

Illustrations

by Spike Mays

Preface and Acknowledgements

We have each written a fair share of the work. Chris provided the first draft, Spike augmented it, and we selected and finished the book together. We could not both be 'I', and the uniform 'we' did not work when writing about one another, so Chris appears in the third person. Spike's own childhood in Bartlow Hamlet, described in his first book *Reuben's Corner*, began when Chris was already an apprentice and living in the adult world of village craftsmen. Most of the pre-1914 events and descriptions of the building trade are his, but we share responsibility for the rest. Our object in writing the book was to pay tribute to old friends of our village, whose clever hands were ousted by mechanisation. Their survivors still plant potatoes on Good Friday and wait until the Cambridge Midsummer Fair before digging the new crop, and never pick gooseberries until Camps Fair, the first Saturday in June.

'Going to Bunkum', for trips to Saffron Walden, was freely used in our young days, though as far as we are aware it is not in the official records. The old English 'bun', meaning squirrel, or 'bune' (reed), and 'cumb' (valley) might have something to do with it: after all, Saffron Walden *is* a medieval town built in a valley which abounded with squirrels and reeds. But we have spelt Bunkum as we have known it for sixty-odd years.

A special word of thanks is due to Brigadier T. F. J. Collins, 'Young Tom', son of the squire of Ashdon Hall, for personal encouragement and assistance in research. Brigadier Collins has served our village in many ways, including getting the sewerage works at Thicko beyond Knox End on the Bartlow road; and he has also privately restored the old Guild Hall to a semblance of its original fabric. Ashdonians are proud too that the Chairman of the County Council should come from the village. His sister Miss Dorothy Collins, who has been active all her life in the interests of the village, lived in Ashdon until 1947 and has recently retired there, resuming her social work for the church, the council, and for the elderly or infirm.

We deeply appreciate the help and encouragement of Mrs E. Beckwith, and Mr and Mrs John Bartram. We offer thanks to Miss Barbara Wright for kind permission to print her letter; and to Mr Bruce Series and the *Cambridge Evening News* for the article on Walter Marsh from the issue of 24 April 1971. In addition, we are indebted to the Editor of *Time and Tide* for permission to reprint from memory the riddle, 'Sedito sali...', which first appeared in an issue of *John O'London's Weekly* (*c.* 1910); to Mr William F. Dooley and the *East Anglian Magazine* for two of Mr Dooley's poems; to Mrs Joan Lay and Benham & Co. Ltd for the extract from 'To Suffolk' by Cecil Lay; to the Estate of A. E. Coppard for 'Forester's song'; and to the Society of Authors as the literary representative of the Estate of John Masefield for the poem 'Land workers'. Finally, acknowledgement is due to the proprietors of the *East Anglian Magazine* who raised no objections to the use of an edited version of Spike's essay, 'An East Anglian Childhood', first published in *The East Anglian Book*, edited by Michael Watkins (1971), which reappears as the Afterword.

CHRISTOPHER KETTERIDGE

1972   SPIKE MAYS

If you'll bear with me I've got things to tell
Of an age long past, but which I knew well;
Of friends of my school years, all plain, simple folk
Who laboured content under their rustic yoke.
I'll tell of the farmhands' cute dodges and skills
That produced golden grain on our bleak windswept hills.

I'll mention our mightiest craftsman's trade,
His strength, expertise and the farm tools he made;
Old Clarky, our blacksmith, and his roaring fire,
Who ingeniously fashioned the stout iron tyre
To clad for long years a wagonwheel rim,
From hunks of base metal he'd hammered in trim.

I'll speak of our Wheelwright who alas! is no more,
His deep, sopping saw-pit and keen whipping saw;
Of our Forester's fellings of ash, elms and oaks
To fashion for wheels sturdy hubs and stout spokes.
Then I'll mention the Painter's fine tricks and cute arts
For protecting so gaily farm wagons and carts.

I'll laud wind-stained thatchers on roof-tops crow high,
Their deep beds of thatch, which oft pleased my eye;
And their 'prentices combing out wheat's golden straw –
Aligned, soaked, roof-ready, yelved flat on the floor;
And sprindles of hazel, split, gleaming and white,
For down-pinning straw and reed, snug and rain-tight.

I'll sing of our Ploughman and Suffolk Punch team,
Of straight furrows they drew beside old Sparks's stream.
Of Shepherds and sheep dogs you soon will be told;
How they tended their flocks within the home fold;
Of the bleats and the baas of young ewes and old rams,
And the frolicsome gambols of springtide's new lambs.

I'll talk of our Hurdler's outmoded skilled trade,
Of Ashdon's own hurdles, most Wally Marsh made;
Of the old Miller's cottage, so high on our hill,
A-nudging the bulk of our grain-grinding mill.
Of the Windmill itself, a magnificent sight,
Built skyward by skills of an Ashdon millwright.

Of our Harnessmaker, the fine Cobbler who
Could fashion or mend hobnailed boots or girl's shoe.
Of our small village Pubs and our gay village Fairs,
Our pair of small shops, both jam-packed with cheap wares;
Then I'll discourse on Chapel, Church, Parsons two,
Who long preached on Sundays on what we 'marn't do'.

I'll praise our two Doctors, our one village Nurse,
Our one body-snatcher – including his hearse –
And salute our grave Sexton, his chill funeral knell –
He dug my friends' graves and pulled well on his bell.
So, after you've read of my old village Friends,
Remember, their story begins, never ends.

CHRISTOPHER KETTERIDGE

1

Five miles from Bunkum

We were both country-bred boys, Chris and I. Chris was born in Ashdon, Essex in 1901, I in Glemsford, Suffolk in 1907. My family came to live in Ashdon in 1914, my mother being a native of the village. It was then that I first met Chris. He was shovelling up batches of mortar in the yard of the Rose and Crown inn, and I, a frail, shy, seven-year old boy in baggy knickers and faded jersey, had come to watch him on my way home from school. Our friendship, which has lasted a lifetime, started at that moment, and now we know each other's memories as if they were our own. Until Chris started courting we spent practically all our leisure together, in the fields, in Mill Meadow, and in Ashdon Mill; roving the country paths and byways, learning about wild life and reading *Macbeth* by candlelight in the mill where the owls hooting around us and dogs whining in distant farmyards lent the right effects for drama. We read Rider Haggard and Edgar Wallace, and invented our own games and pastimes, from making the first cat's-whisker wireless set in the village to a circus game which we played with great dexterity down Mill Lane, using rubber quoit rings and hazel wands.

Chris's father, York Ketteridge, was a master builder. He represented the fifth generation of bricklayers in and around the village. His great-great-grandfather, born in the 1760s, his grandfather James and great-uncles William and Henry, were all well known in Ashdon in their time. The parish accounts of St Mary's, Bartlow include payments made to 'William Kitteridge, stone wall to churchyard as per agreement £23 0s 0d' (1827) and 'Kitteridge bricklayer £9 18s 0d' (1842). This evidently referred to great-uncle William and perhaps Henry too.

York Ketteridge, a superb craftsman, took pains to train his six sons in his own high standards of workmanship. The eldest, Marmaduke (Duke for short), worked in Cambridge as foreman for a private firm, where in due course Albert joined him. York and Edwin mostly worked away from home and Chris sometimes went with them, as happened in 1924-5 when they reconstructed the barracks of Catterick Camp in Yorkshire. The fifth son Jack was Chris's companion until 1914, but he died a prisoner-of-war in 1918. All the brothers except Chris joined up during the 1914-18 war. He was only seventeen when it ended. The girls, Kate, Alice, Penelope, Mabel and Annie, were older than Chris, and Bess the youngest of the family was born in 1906. Of the twelve Annie, Bess and Chris are still alive and Annie still lives in Ashdon.

Chris faced up his first brick when he was nine on the house of Captain Revill, which his father and York and Edwin were rebuilding after a fire. 'The Little House' is still there on the Radwinter Road, almost rubbing shoulders with old Clarky Cooper's smithy. He left school at thirteen, having won a scholarship he was unable to take up, and became an apprentice in his father's building trade. The Ketteridge family have left indelible marks on the village, but Chris himself has personally built only one pair of cottages there. In 1926 he married Agnes Green, who was then working at Bartlow, and she bore him three sons, Dennis, Peter and Alan. Agnes's family were in sheep, and we have a photo of her uncle Arthur Grewes of Little Sampford, one of three brothers who were all shepherds, like their father. When Chris retired in 1968 he moved only a few miles away to Great Wratting, Suffolk. Thus his knowledge of Ashdon parish stretches from hearsay handed down to him until the present day.

My father John Mays was at various times a postman, a soldier, a gardener and a farm labourer. My brother Leslie, my sister Audrey and I were all born at my parents' first home at Glemsford, Suffolk. We moved from there to Helions Bumpstead and then to Bartlow Hamlet, Ashdon, where we rented the cottage next door to my maternal grandparents, Reuben and Susannah Ford, for one and ninepence a week. It was my mother's birthplace. The two cottages were Ketteridge-built, dating from the 1850s, and were owned by Alfred Hagger who farmed Overhall Farm. I lived in this tied cottage for nine years until I left to join the army at the age of sixteen.

During those years from late 1914 to early 1924 Ashdon was a self-contained community, still remote because of the lack of transport. It lies five miles east of Saffron Walden and seven miles west of Haverhill, Suffolk, on a section of the Roman road between Cambridge and Ipswich. Saffron Walden, the market town which derives its name from growing saffron, was locally known as Bunkum. No one knew the origin of that name, but all knew its other Ashdon nickname, God-help-us, dated from times when the town was plague-stricken and folk bound for the market crossed themselves before entering.

At the turn of the century the only way to reach these market towns was on foot or by horse and cart. Our villagers lived in an old-fashioned world of oil lamps, wells, home baking, poaching, large families and skilful housekeeping. Almost everything was handmade, including the tools they used. Most of the men were farmhands, serving as ploughmen, horsekeepers, stockmen, shepherds, hedgers, ditchers, harvesters and thatchers. To supply other needs there were blacksmiths, harnessmakers, foresters, wheelwrights, hurdlemakers, cobblers, butchers, bakers, grocers, teachers, doctors, midwives and, of course, publicans and parsons.

The centre of the village was Crown Hill, where women gathered at the pump for drinking water and gossip. Here too was the Rose and Crown, the old Cromwellian coaching inn. Clusters of picturesque cottages, some clay and wattle, but most of them thatched, lay along the two main streets, the Ashdon-Radwinter and the Saffron Walden-Ashdon-Bartlow roads. Lesser roads, lanes, cart tracks and footpaths led from distant fields, farms and woods, alongside ditches, hedgerows and allotments, up hill and down dale. Nine square miles of rich farmlands and woods, forming a continuation of the East Anglian Heights. Most of the workers' cottages were built in the valley beside the Bourne, the stream which cuts the parish in two on its northward course to the Granta and eventually to the Cam. Farms and outbuildings were dotted about the hilltops. In addition to the village itself, the parish embraced a hamlet, endless Ends, five major farms and many minor ones. There was a church and a chapel, two Sunday schools and a day school, two shops, five pubs, and the squire's mansion, Walton's Park, which was entirely destroyed by fire in February 1954, and since rebuilt.

The site of Walton's Park is part of the land called Stevington in Domesday Book, but its present name dates from 1269 when Richard de Walton leased it. There was an archway by the side of a pond in the rookery at the rear of the sixteenth-century house which was said to be the entrance of an underground passage. We boys were told that it led to Ashdon Church two miles away, but we were never able to explore it. There were also medieval fishponds which rose one above the other in the grounds. To the south of Walton's is the home farm, formerly Ashdon Place and now Place Farm. Adjoining it, near the stockyards, is a great barn, framed in oak and tiled, which has seven bays with aisles like the nave of a church. It is a building of remarkable workmanship and beauty. As boys it filled us with wonder; but for me the wonder wore off when I used to mix cattle bait in one of the bays.

Chris and I used to explore together the Bartlow Hills, on the borders of Cambridgeshire. Originally there were five of these curious humps, but one was removed in 1865 for the proposed track of the Great Shelford-Marks Tey railway. When we were confronted by the first tall conical-shaped mound draped with shrubs and saplings and, a little beyond, by the other three hills half hidden by woodland growth, we sensed a strange quietening influence. They reminded us of bygone ages and men long dead, as indeed is apt for they are the graves of warriors. The tradition persists that they date from the battle between Edmund Ironside and Canute, but excavations in the mid-nineteenth century disclosed first-century Roman walled graves containing glass ornaments and decorated bronzes and enamels. They are reputedly the largest burial mounds in Europe, the greatest being 40 ft high by 145 ft long.

I sang in the choir of our parish church, All Saints, which was founded in Saxon times. I was baptised at its ancient font, with its trumpet-shaped wooden cover painted with lilies, and I have witnessed many baptisms there since. Boys used to climb to the bell loft by the spiral staircase where the stones were almost worn away by centuries of use. Not that the bell loft was used then, for the timbers and the tower structure had deteriorated over the years and the tenor bell was badly cracked. For over a century the bells had been tolled by ropes manipulated from a wooden frame in the vestry, but on Sunday evenings 'Thatcher' Freeman used to play the evening hymn on those old bells – 'The day Thou gavest Lord is ended'. In 1969 the cracked bell was recast, new bells were added, the tower was strengthened, and new floors and stairs made. It was a fine moment when those bells rang a peal for the first time. The organ, which had a wonderful tone, was also restored then. In my day it was worked by bellows and pumped by a well-worn, worm-eaten handle. Sometimes Johnny Purkis would fall asleep at his pumping post on Sunday mornings, to the great annoyance of Mabel Eason, our organist.

All Saints' living was in the patronage of the Rev. C. H. Brocklebank of neighbouring Bartlow, a multi-millionaire by repute. He occasionally preached at our church, and I well remember that sermon when he chose for his text, 'The rich man at his castle, the poor man at his gate'. He placed his hands on the ledge of the pulpit, leaned slightly forward, and with a bland smile on his ruddy face demanded, 'Now what are you going to do about that?' We all liked Mr Brocklebank. One of his chief interests was the breeding and training of greyhounds and his ambition was to win the Waterloo Cup with one of them. We used to watch them coursing over our windswept hills with magnificent speed, and felt a bit sorry that he never achieved his aim. We too had our disappointments in life and here was a parson with one we understood. We came to know several of the rectors of All Saints. The first of our time was the Rev. D. B. R. Banham, a strict, austere, but much respected man. His two daughters shared the task of training the choir, and made a good job of it. His stipend was a princely £1,500, but he gave one tenth to the parish and held only one collection a month. Compared with this, the vicar of Saffron Walden drew £150 a year, out of which he paid two assistant curates. Mr Banham was succeeded in 1915 by the Rev. F. C. Hartley, an ex-naval padre who disciplined us with a rod of iron.

Mrs Brocklebank supported the Waifs & Strays Home, better known today as a Church of England Children's Society home. Its timber and plaster structure was encased in red brick after the First World War. The Ketteridge family, Chris included, did this work, using bricks from the private brickworks on Lord Braybrooke's estate at Audley End, which were the last bricks produced there. In its original form it was an orphanage for boys maintained by the Church and run by a kindly and much loved matron, Miss Whitehead. Most of the boys wrote to her regularly after they had left and had found positions in the church or the services. This rambling red brick house is about a quarter of a mile from the centre of the village and is built on glebe lands. It is surrounded by well-cultivated gardens.

Behind the church itself is a cluster of timber-framed, two-storeyed buildings which were built in about 1480. The upper one, which was once the Guild Hall, later became a poor house tenanted for rents. The older people still refer to the others as a 'bit of the owd wukkus', and to the former Guild Hall as the 'housen of the wukkus master'.

Nonconformists, who outnumbered Anglicans, worshipped

in the large Baptist chapel on the Radwinter road. Under the floorboards of the rostrum lay a large tank of holy water reserved for baptism by total immersion. It was impolitely described as 'that owd sheep dip'. Some of us Anglican boys would occasionally gate-crash baptisms in order to witness the immersion of our school friends or adults; but the Baptists were always tolerant and would welcome visitors to their church, their temperance meetings, bun fights or magic lantern shows. Return visits to All Saints on the other hand were regarded by the Church of England congregation as the deplorable antics of devil-dodgers.

Pastor Smith, the Baptist minister, lived at the Manse a little way outside the village, up a narrow and very stony lane. His livelihood was precarious because he was dependent on the generosity of his flock. Although they came in droves to his chapel as a place of refuge, or a place to discuss their problems, they were not the sort of people to have much money to spare.

Ministers of both church and chapel visited even the humblest of cottagers on missions of spiritual enlightenment. Their parishioners were not always pleased. . .

'They can all use theer owd jars (jaws), an' can talk the hind leg orf a donkey, but I ain't sin one yet as could knock a clout nail into a bit of sorft wood . . . Parson's gotter gard'ner. Can't dig a bloody spit hisself, but when he gits up in that owd pulpit, all starched an' ironed an' sashed, yewed think he got the harvest in hisself. Set up there a-hollering an' a-blarin' fer as long as he can git away oo it.'

Long and baffling words from educated tongues were out of place in village pulpits. One labourer with ten children was asked by a parson why he had a child each year.

'My missus has 'em, not me, metty. She gits 'em same's ever'body else. I look arter 'em, but I ain't never sure if they're all MY. Now, if yew owd parsons'd put yewer trousers on same way round as yewer collars, an' stop a-visitin' when we're out a-wukkin', mebbe we wouldn't hev so many.'

21

But these were the exception. Parsons opportunely arriving at meal times would be fed. If it was the Baptist parson, and the cottager was good at growing vegetables, a large basket was invariably filled for him.

Easter brought the faithful in their best clothes to the lily and palm-bedecked church of All Saints. Seating was according to means. Those with the most were nearest to the priest, those with the least were well to the back. It was said that pews could be purchased. In the chapel there was greater fervour and no status seating, and loud interjections of 'Praise the Lord', hosts of heartfelt 'Hallelujahs' and drawn-out 'AAAmens'. Chapel-goers were teetotallers (on Sundays), wore blue temperance badges and went straight home to their Sunday dinners. Anglicans usually gravitated to the Fox or the Rose and Crown after Matins – 'ter git the dust outer me throat, an' let the batter pudden rise and the gravy thicken'.

Some older men went so far as to say that organised religion was partly responsible for the deterioration of morals and ethics. Years ago villagers used to show their disapproval in a practical way. The culprit may have been a common busy-body with a long nose for prying, or a malicious tongue for slander. If the prying and gossiping brought distress, action might well be taken, but it was usually reserved for men found in adultery with married women, or seducers of young girls. When word had gone round retribution was swift and sure. Menfolk would band together to make 'rough music'; each taking a saucepan, kettle, frying pan, or something likely to produce a din when struck with metal. Some took rattles like those we used for bird scaring. There was bound to be one with a bull roarer, a flat board with sharply serrated edges, cut to an oval and tied to a cord. When swung vigorously round the 'musician's' head it would give off a deafening roar. After dark the men would stealthily take up position surrounding the culprit's house. At a signal pandemonium would break out. The culprit knew better than to show himself. The din would continue until the demonstrators were tired or hoarse from cat-calling. It was intended, and usually happened, that the culprit would then leave the village.

The tribal feeling at the heart of the village is less evident now, perhaps because there is not so much need to stick together in a modern society. But the keenest loss is that of our own breed of craftsmen. These artificers of the old stamp knew their raw materials and how to use them, and had the everyday humour of countrymen born and bred. Chris was already learning from them while I was at school.

2

Of clay and wattles made

Past farm buildings and cottages known as 'Thicker' (Thicko), half way to Bartlow, 'Brick'll' (Brick Kiln) was a series of long low shelters, a pair of brick buildings, and some huts made from oak. There were two kilns and a deep circular pit called the Pug Mill. In the pit was a wooden bladed paddle wheel rotated by horse power which ground brick earth, freeing the yellow clay from stones and impurities as it was doused with water. Raw bricks, drying and maturing in the air, were stacked to capacity in the low shelters, in readiness for burning in the kiln.

This old brickyard was a thriving industry, and many tons of clay were converted into building units, as witnessed by the vast excavations. For many years the yard was owned and run by Bell & Sons, whose bricks were distinguished by the 'B' deeply imprinted into each concave frog. At the end of the last century a small frog was introduced, and bricks were thinner and longer than the modern variety, and of varying colour according to the degrees of heat in the baking process, ranging from a pinky-yellow through a series of deeper reds to near black. Their shapes were attractively uneven. Ashdon bricks were sought after and used far beyond the parish boundaries, and many buildings still standing were constructed from them, such as the cottages on Church Hill. Some of the brickmen survived until after the Great War.

Old Frankie Barrett who lived in Dorvis Lane was a ganger. Sam W. Chapman, a brickmaker known to all as Captain, and towards the end of his life, Wilkes, because he had worked as a tyer for John Wilkes, a well-known hay and straw merchant, worked with three strangely named brothers Smith – Wuddy, Fuller and Pudden. They had much to impart about the making

of bricks to anyone sufficiently interested in listening. Frankie
was short, stocky, unbelievably rugged, honest and conscientious. He always wore a red handkerchief tightly knotted at
his throat, its two ends fastened to the sides of his web braces,
a corduroy suit and billycock hat set jauntily on his head. He
was husky and gritty of speech, and without the least encouragement would launch into precise and prolonged descriptions.

'Yes, we used to have a hoss an' cart when we were a-diggin'
out the brick earth, an' we used to load up the owd cart till we
had enough to fill the Pug Mill. Then o' course, we had to take
the owd hoss owt an' then harness him to the arm o' the mill,
ye see.'

What did *pug* mean, and why did the clay have to be
ground?

'Pug! Why, that's the plastic clay, bor, the brick earth. We
had to grind it to make it wukkable, loike, an' git all the stone
out. When we chucked the water on it went all sloppy, an' as
the mill turned the stones wukked outer the soides. Most o' the
water drained away when we filled the bins with pug. That
had to lay there a day or two afore we could move it to the
mouldin' shed, an' that's where owd Captain done the
mouldin'. Ain't you never seen anybody a-mouldin' bricks,
then? Well, you hev a mould what's lined with metal, jest the
size of a brick, an' the bottom on't is raised a bit for the frog.
You picks up a lump o' pug, bang it down hard into the
mould an' fill it. Then you pick up the mould with the pug in
it an' jounces it a time or two on the bench jest to make sure
she's full. When she's nice an' full you take a strike, thasser
bit o' wood, an' cut the pug off clean at the sides. Then you
pick up a wood pallet what's a mite bigger'n the mould, an'
lays it on the mould. You turn the whole lot upsides down
an' let it mould off. An' there's yer brick, moulded, frog an'
all.'

All the time Frankie mimed merrily away, going through all
the movements he had made almost instinctively over the years.

He demonstrated how raw bricks were stacked in a specially made wheelbarrow with capacious base but no sides to facilitate unloading, and wheeled to the 'hacks' (the low shelters) and stacked there in such a way that the air played freely round them; and in due course they were placed inside the big brick kilns, with fuel packed between them, to be fired, the whole being ignited through holes spaced opposite each other along the sides.

'You've allus gotter hev two kilns, otherwise you'd be held up, loike. While the one's a-coolin' off after burnin', you can be a-loadin' t'other ready. Crowdin' on it.'

Chris, two of his brothers and his father, rebuilt a country house nearby, and in excavating for the swimming pool a vast amount of yellow clay was removed, immediately identified by Old Wilkes as, 'Wholly beautiful brick earth. Best I ever seen!' Chris had an old brick mould which Frankie Barrett gave him as a memento, and Wilkes was pressed into service. With great satisfaction he turned out a number of perfectly moulded bricks which were conveyed to the Cambridge brickworks of Watts to burn in one of their kilns. Chris was chosen to lay them.

The builder was jack and master of all trades; he had to be. Bricklayer-mason, plasterer, carpenter, painter and decorator, and often plumber too, his tool-kit was large and varied and whatever the need he rose to it. His routine work was maintaining farm buildings and cottages, including derelict thatched cottages which often had to be made habitable for a worker, and these would be completely restored. Most farmers employed a handyman to cope with the repair of fences, cleaning drains, and sundry other jobs, but for major repairs the builder was called in.

The squire relied on him for services beyond the scope of his staff, such as building a damp course, which only an expert could accomplish successfully. Several courses of bricks had to be cut out from the thickness and length of the wall and a double course of properly lapped slates embedded in it, without disturbing the structure or causing any subsidence. This was carried out on many of the older buildings threatened with rising damp.

Rebuilding high chimney stacks involved a mass of scaffolding and the careful demolition of the old stacks, and if the squints and splays used in the ornamental brickwork were not readily available they were cut from standard bricks, a job calling for special skills and tools.

A subsidence in the section of a wall would incur underpinning and the insertion of a new foundation, while altering the façade of a building might demand the erection of different sized windows, and always without too obvious signs that the fabric had been tampered with. When a boundary wall collapsed during a spell of frost the old material would be as far as possible utilised in rebuilding it, and most bricklayers were expert at laying the flint in bays between brick piers. This technique produced a variety of pleasing patterns, and was specialist's work, as many an amateur has discovered to his cost.

North Essex abounds with flint boundary walls and the task of rebuilding them was familiar to the village builder. Plenty of other buildings and churches too are made from a large percentage of flint infilling between quoins of Barnack stone and window jambs of moulded clunch.

The builder undertook many roofing jobs, after having to strip tiles and laths to take new battens, insulating the roof with layers of soft hay or moss as he retiled. Tiles loosely laid on a

bed of moss expanded and contracted in extremes of temperature, and any moisture inadvertently penetrating the roof thus
escaped. Alternatively, the tiles could be bedded in lime
mortar, a method serving the same end but liable to cause
broken tiles, and therefore not recommended.

Men were carefully trained in their jobs. Master craftsmen
handed down their skills, father to son, for many generations
and naturally the sons inherited the feel of tools. It was their
like who built the much admired old cottages, the great barns
and cattle sheds, rambling farmhouses and mansions, school
and chapel.

The brick culverts spanning the stream Bourne which
support the highway – originally intended for horse-drawn
vehicles – have borne hundreds of tons of motor traffic, a
testimonial to the builders, illiterate though they may have
been. The Fox and the Rose and Crown, both sixteenth-
century inns, were the work of local men, forbears of the
Ketteridge craftsmen.

Periodically a very necessary but highly uncomfortable task
was performed for the baker, the renewing of the lining of
his furnace. Old fire lumps had to be cut and replaced with new
ones, and in addition a man would often have to work inside
the oven renewing brick paving in the floor. The oven was no
more than eighteen inches from floor to crown and the terrific
heat prevented him from staying inside more than a minute at
a time, after which he would come out quickly, streaming with
sweat and gasping for air. In he would go again, lying prone
to do his work, his body blocking out the light and his legs
protruding from the oven door. The heat precluded the use of
a candle. This work was done in between baking times, but
even at weekends when there was no baking the oven could
not be cooled sufficiently to make conditions bearable. Whenever Chris repaired furnace and oven, which he has done
several times, usually a severe cold followed the ordeal.

Portland cement was considered too brittle for most work.
Builders pinned their faith and reputation on mortar mixed

from rock lime and sand, a bonding agent used in the construction of Norman castles and churches which have survived. Lime obtained locally came in lumps as hard as stone which had to be reduced to powder by slaking. They were piled on the banker, or mixing space, saturated with water and covered with sand to keep the heat in. Thick clouds of steam soon rose from the visibly expanding heap as it was transformed into fine powder. It was then mixed and sieved, enough sand added, and knocked up with water into a buttery consistency. This mortar is tough and resilient, and was used in bricklaying and external plastering. For the setting coat on internal plaster a mixture of two parts pure lime putty to one part fine sharp sand was generally used. To obtain this putty, lump-lime was slaked in a tank of water and as it heated it was stirred to the consistency of cream, then strained through a very fine sieve into a pit or bin, left to solidify and then cut out like butter. It had a variety of uses. Hair mortar, also used in plastering, prevented cracks appearing. Lime was put in the tank with water, as before, then poured into a circle of sand, well beaten ox hair added and raked in with a long-handled rake, and the sand gradually mixed in. This strong mortar was used on ceilings and framed partitions, but if used in external work a dusting of Portland cement might be applied before plastering. Egyptian mortar, seldom used except for patching original plaster, was made from clay mixed with prodigious quantities of straw and chaff. Clay is subject to a high rate of shrinkage and is liable to crack when drying out, and the straw and chaff to some extent remedied this. Patent plasters were almost unheard of and would probably have been regarded with suspicion by the old craftsmen.

In Ashdon the builder shared a yard with the wheelwright. This was Charles Cooper, senior, who was part wheelwright, part builder. His yard was extensive, with many buildings for storing materials and ancillary plant. The adjoining smithy which also belonged to him was run by his son Clarky. A portly John Bull with rubicund face and Gladstonian whiskers, old Charles was a deacon of the Baptist chapel. He neither smoked nor drank and rarely smiled. His habitual expression was solemn, as befitted an undertaker. His clothing was sombre, and he always wore a hat in the street. In the workshop he wore a voluminous apron.

He employed two workmen, Walter (Starchy) and Jim Williams, father and son, who did most of the outside jobs. They were often seen pushing their handcart about the village, laden with ladders and the paraphernalia of their mixed trades. They usually went about in clouds of smoke, all fragrant from their pipes after careful fillings of 'Golden Honeydew' tobacco. When Charles Cooper died Starchy Williams carried on the business, until late in life, when he sold his premises and erected a carpenter's workshop at Church Hill. The villagers thought it appropriate that he was called 'Starchy', if only for his professional dealings with the 'stiffs'.

York Ketteridge also undertook work for Charles Cooper, and none of the principal property owners of the district would have dreamt of employing anyone else. York was dedicated. He never made money for his family, but lived up to the tradition of doing his job correctly in every way, and his sons were equally conscientious – it was their heritage, their duty.

My brother Leslie Mays always enjoyed walking across the fields with York. It was good exercise, for York loped along at a furious lick; his legs seemed to shoot from under him to land almost too far ahead, but hitting the ground just in time to stop him toppling forward. Les used to jog-trot to keep up, not to miss a word of his language, for York was one of the finest swearers in Ashdon, and recounting his 'wicked wuds' was one exercise the hamlet boys enjoyed. But he was a most kind and understanding man who knew about wheats, their differences in height, colour and yield. He would snatch a couple of near-ripened ears, rub them in his horny hands to shed the husks, then blow into his cupped hands to winnow husks from grain. Husks clung to his whiskers as he tossed the grain into his mouth. 'Wheat is life, boy. Don't let no silly bugger tell you different!' And then a gun went off in the distance, and another shot, and there was Rodwell the keeper taking shots at wood-pigeons. 'Silly owd sod,' said York. 'Oughter hev more sense, walkin' about arter things what fly.'

York and his sons had much to do with the repair and maintenance of village cottages. Essex is renowned for its thatched cottages, constructed of local timber, plastered with clay by the wattle and daub method, and thatched with straw or Norfolk reeds. Little real attention was given to the shape and symmetry as long as the timber was sound.

Due to the shape of the timber cill it was rarely possible to prepare the foundation first. Instead, the ground cill – cut to required lengths to encompass the entire plan of the walls, and joined and pinned together by half-lap joints – was packed up slightly clear of the ground and a foundation built into the void which was filled in with a mixture of bricks and flint stones laid in lime mortar. One had only to see the undulations of some old cottage foundations to realise why this method was adopted.

When supported in position, mortice holes were marked in the cill and cut to take the main posts and intermediate stud-work of the wall. The top ends of these timbers were cut into tenons which, in turn, were fitted into corresponding mortices of the gut plate supporting the stout main beam across the centre of the room – perhaps the sturdiest and most familiar feature of cottage ceilings. On this beam were fixed joists, either by mortice and tenon jointing, or by stout wooden pegs; then all was ready for laying the floorboards.

The main beam was usually secured to the gut plate by stout iron dogs, a system of stapling and bolting. The iron dogs, nails, bolts and other pieces of ironwork used in construction were hammered by the village blacksmith.

To stop the upright rocking in the wind strong diagonal timber braces were fixed to the assembled studwork. While the timber work was prepared and erected by the carpenters, another man and his mate built the wide chimney breast to house the kitchen range and the horseshoe-shaped domed brick oven. Across the eight-foot wide opening they placed a great elm beam, the bressummer, and on this support built the flue, tapering it slowly and evenly to the dimensions of a finished chimney stack to protrude through the roof. The oven was constructed with an arched recess beneath it to take the embers from the furnace. The flue above the bressummer would be pargeted as the work proceeded, a process of facing it up with mortar composed of lime and cow dung. This mixture, impervious to smoke, clung tenaciously to the brickwork and was universally used. Proof of its powers of adherence has often been found by workmen repairing or demolishing chimney stacks after a hundred years. 'That owd parge', as the workmen called it, still clung to the flue breasts, virtually unstained. Pargeting was also an art, decorative as well as preservative, and in Church Street, Saffron Walden there are ancient houses near the church with wonderful examples of this craftsmanship.

From ceiling level the side walls were built up on the gut plate, in the same manner as the ground floor, to the height required to support the roof plate which might spring direct from the gut plate, though this would depend upon resources. Usually walls were continued for two or three more feet, otherwise the bedrooms would be low and cramped indeed. Fixed as before by mortice and tenon joints, the roof plate was prepared, a series of joggle joints cut along the entire length. These indentations, some three or four inches wide, were cut horizontally to leave a sharp-edged ridge in the centre of which the square cut of the rafter fitted snugly into place, both securely fixed by a stout oak peg.

Rafters were fitted in pairs, the tops by half-lap joints secured by wooden pins. It was seldom that a ridge-board was employed, but a pole was sometimes secured beneath the apex of the rafters as a stiffener. Such roofs were necessarily con-structed to a very steep pitch for the eventual covering with thatch. At ceiling height, cross beams called collars were fixed across the rafters, and on these the laths would be laid and nailed. Provision was made for dormer windows in the roof, their cheeks built up and roofed over to blend with the rest of the structure. Then, with the framework of the roof to form a working scaffold, the bricklayer completed his building of the chimney stack to the appropriate height above the finished thatch. Bricks used in this construction were invariably made from local clay, and sometimes salvaged from derelict buildings. Either the carpenter or the handyman now formed openings for windows and doors and built up the gable ends with stout timber studwork, and perhaps a frame for another roof window in the upper bedroom.

Inside the cottage stacked ready for use lay quantities of riven laths, all centrally split ash poles. They would be secured with iron nails to the uprights of the studwork. When this 'cladding' process was completed, two or three coats of clay reinforced with straw and chaff would be applied over the whole area to form a dry and perfectly windproof covering.

If, however, it was decided to reveal the beauty of the old timber, the wattle and daub method would be adopted. This involved plastering the clay compound only between the oak studs. To 'fasten' the background required ingenuity. A series of holes would be bored two feet apart in the centre of the inside faces of the timber. On the side of the stud opposite these holes long grooves were cut. Lengths of hazel wood cut to size, their ends trimmed and pointed, were inserted in the holes, the other ends forced into the opposite grooves. When all the wood was in position it presented the appearance of many ladders with widely-spaced rungs. To these were lashed more hazel wands placed vertically and close together, filling the space to be plastered. Usually the binding or lashing material used was the long, tough fibrous stem of the wild clematis, commonly called Old Man's Beard. On this sturdy framework the plasterers quickly and expertly covered the surface areas with a mixture of clay, chaff and straw. But it was only upon the whims and fancies of owners that cottage exteriors received this treatment. Old countrymen and the weatherwise were more concerned with protection than decoration and preferred timbers plastered all over. Today one sees near this type of cottage small ponds or depressions – positive indications that clay used in cladding and plastering was excavated on the spot.

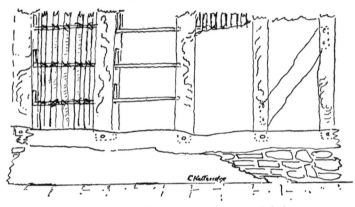

When the exterior had been weather-proofed the carpenter, usually the village wheelwright, made stout-ledged doors and window sashes, planing and pegging, and whistling as he worked, while his mate cut panes of glass and knocked up putty from whiting and linseed oil. Mounds of wheat straw would be dumped at strategic places and the thatcher and his mate arrived, swathing themselves in sacking, particularly round their knees for protection against the ladder rungs; and in a comparatively short time the roof would be covered with a combed and trimmed straw thatch, which made the cottage warm in winter and delightfully cool on the hottest of summer days.

Then the carpenter would start his interior work, laying oak floorboards to bedrooms, and building each step of the tortuous stair which gave access to them.

The same mixture of clay, chaff and straw was used for plastering the walls and lean-to ceilings of the bedrooms. The cottage seemed to be filled with happy men of various trades with but one object in mind; to build a good house. By this time the lower floors had been covered with paving bricks, laid on a bed of sand and chalk and fully consolidated. Into the base of the chimney opening the bricklayer would build the iron fire basket. The cottage was nearing completion. Its clay-coated walls, now dried out, were given several coats of lime wash; white on the interior to give light, and sometimes dyed with the red juice of sloes and black damsons to provide 'Constable pink' for the outer walls.

Another type of structure for cottages with solid walls, built from blocks of clay by a process practised in eastern countries, is called 'clay lump' or 'clay bats'. Well wetted clay and straw prepared 'cob fashion' was formed into bricks in wooden moulds and left to dry out thoroughly in wind and sun. Mostly a foot long, six inches wide and deep, they made excellent bricks and were used in localities where sturdy timbers were hard to come by, or when artisans of timber-framing were not available.

First, the foundation was laid, of brick, or a composite of brick and flint, to take the clay bats. This foundation presented none of the uneven contours and undulations of the oak cills. Walls were built to the height of the roof plate, and the surfaces generally coated with a clay and straw mixture as an added protection.

The carpenter would erect the roof as before; cutting out all his timbers and shaping them with hand tools, saw, adze and plane. Provided damp was kept from the clay bats after they had dried their life was incalculable.

Cottages constructed by this method had the merit of more coolness in very hot weather, and more warmth and cosiness in winter than the timber-framed thatched cottages. Although a clay mixture was adequate protection against the elements, it tended to crumble when exposed to intermittent heat.

The bricklayer built a chimney, a domed oven, and perhaps a brick copper as well. Named because the furnace pan was made of this metal, a 'copper' was a much prized possession of the housewife who boasted one, usually built in a corner, with a connecting flue running to the chimneypiece. Sometimes this was improved upon by constructing an outbuilding at the rear of the cottage, to house two brick coppers. And in some remote corner of the garden, half hidden by trees and shrubs, would be the privy, built over a deep cess-pit.

The heavy Essex clay was always an important building material. Farmhouses and cottages owe much of their cosiness to the thick layers of common clay which protect the timbers; and the famous bread ovens retained their heat from thick coatings plastered over their crowns. But Essex 'brick clay' or 'brick earth', as old bricklayers call it, is yellow, and from it was made the red brick common to Essex. This clay is very soft, with a total absence of chalk or stone and, as Frankie Barrett used to say, 'it can be dug out like butter'. Many a village boasted a flourishing brickyard, and granaries, stables and the open-fronted sheds of farmers' stockyards were built of brick made from this yellow clay, which was used in the construction of pantiles, ridge tiles, valley tiles, hip and bonnet tiles, to cover the roofs of farm buildings. Agricultural drain pipes were also made from this yellow clay.

In some parts of Essex adjoining clay belts, thick chalk deposits lie just beneath the soil, holding quantities of black flint. Both chalk and flint were much used in building. From the chalk, or limestone, came the lime which was added to sand to make mortar for bricklaying. Black flint built into cottage walls in conjunction with various patterns of red brick made pleasing colour contrasts in ingenious systems of panelling. Such cottages have a very warm appearance, but do not withstand the elements so well, nor do they catch the eye as do the clay walls of dazzling white and warm Constable pink. Yet the 'brick and stoners' have a charm of their own, especially when you live in a pair of them with your parents and grand-parents, and they are framed by Keeper's Cottage and Walt's Cottage, both of clay and thatch, and standing at Reuben's Corner; when round the little porches there are trailings of flaming japonica, and round the door and windows old English tea roses, Maiden's Blush, and tendrils of sweet-scented honeysuckle; when they were built by the ancestors of your best friend, and the house martins come and build their clay nests there – over all the years.

3

Wheelwright, blacksmith, cobbler and all . . .

Plump pompous Charles Cooper, part builder, part wheel-wright, also functioned as village undertaker, making sturdy coffins of elm and oak which his son Clarky boasted were 'guaranteed to larst a bloody lifetime'. But his main work was the making and repairing of tumbrils, dog-carts, wagons, wheelbarrows and wheels; combining carpentry, building, smithing, paint-making and painting.

Two-storeyed and well lit by windows glazed with oddly assorted panes, his workshop was enormous. The working bench occupied the length of the ground floor, where tools of all sorts lay to hand – bow saws, pad saws, rip saws and coping saws – each with its purpose. There were all kinds of knives, planes, spokeshaves, long-handled augers, and endless templates. Some planes were concave, some convex; try planes, jack planes, block planes, smoothers; and chisels of all widths and queer distortions stood in racks. There were sledge hammers, ball-payne hammers, block-and-nail hammers of the Warrington pattern, beechwood mallets, and always a big mallet made of apple wood and bound with iron hoops, the beetle, used for driving in stakes; and iron wedges for splitting hard, twisted-grain timber. The wheelwright's oldest tool, the adze, is razor-edged and a good man could true rough timber with it as expertly as a carpenter with a plane, but its main use was taking off the bulk of unwanted wood and roughly shaping the work.

All these tools were kept clean, sharp, oiled and set. Setting involves careful alignment of saw teeth, slightly twisting from the blade, one to the off, one to the near, with pincer pliers, or punched with hammer and centre punch . . . 'A saw ain't set proper unless yew can drop a needle twixt the fust few teeth an' make it roide down the lot without a-stoppin'.'

Sharpening is an art in itself; by using slim, triangular files each tooth receives individual attention, first one side, then the next, and if no needle was handy the human eye was brought into play for sighting down the rows of teeth.

Beechwood, close-grained and durable, was ideal for marking out felloes ('fellies' in Suffolk), the segments of ashwood which fit together in a circle to form the outer circumference of the wheel. Before they are joined together and spoked to the hub, the felloes are trued with adze, spoke-shave and plane. The wheelwright's apprentice shaped the gently curved felloes from the ashwood held fast in the vice, the tempered blade of his plane sounding a crisp note as the thin shavings curled away.

Upstairs to the whirr and rattle of the turning lathe a block of wych elm was shaped into the hub of a wheel, by a foot treadle. The twelve spokes were fitted in the yard outside, on a triangular trestle. Over all pervaded the clean smells of new wood and linseed oil.

Trimmed boles of oak, ash and elm lay waiting to be cut into planks and scantlings in the sawpit, an open-sided roofed shed, 6 ft deep by 4 ft wide and from 12 ft to 20 ft long, with boarded sides to prevent falling earth, and a duck-boarded base. This was usually flooded in winter and was then a most unpleasant place to work in. Baulks laid across the width supported the timber to be sawn, which was placed length-wise and metal dogs attached to prevent rolling. One sawyer stood on the log and hauled up the long heavy double-handed saw from his mate in the pit. Every bit of wood used by the wheelwright had to be sawn in this way. The planks were laid flat and sawn in the same manner, except that a finer-toothed saw was used. This heavy work was performed many years before the wood was taken into construction. Planks and cuts were always separated by battens to allow free air during storage, and there was always a good supply of seasoned timber. It was more than likely that timber in use had been sawn by the previous generation.

For making felloes ash from hedgerows was preferred to ash taken from woods and copses. Wych elm was a favourite wood for making hubs; with its twisted and distorted grain it was almost impossible to split, even with the beetle and iron wedges.

Selecting timber was a cunning business. Elder wheelwrights would walk mile upon mile beside thick hedges, making notes, sometimes blaze-marking trees which took their fancy, and a particularly suitable one might be bought there and then, even though it would not be fit for felling for ten years or more. This applied more to ash and elm than to oak, always tough whether it grew in wood or hedge and favoured for coachwork. Some local farmers preferred white poplar, 'They non-quiverin', non-splinterin' aspens, bor, high as the sky, straight as a die.' In an open space in the yard on a circular metal plate sunk level with surrounding surfaces, steel tyres were heated prior to fitting to the wooden rims. Tyre making was all done by hand, hammer and eye. Shavings, woodcuts and other fuel were piled round it and ignited. Heating caused the tyre to expand, to be slipped over the wheel, and when cool it fitted tightly and immovably. This process was known as 'shrinking on'.

Wagons and tumbrils were painted in colours usually chosen generations before; traditionally each farmer kept to his own. It was simple for us to determine the owner of a field by the colour of the farm carts. The Haggers of Overhall Farm used a deep blue for generations. Ashdon Place Farm had used light blue, but when the Luddingtons came to Walton's Park and its farms they brought with them their own colour from Cambridgeshire, beige. Wheelwrights bought the pigments from the county town and ground and mixed their own paints. First they went over every inch of woodwork with smoothers and fillers, then on would go a priming of white or pink, a coat of flat, and two good coats of colour, and to finish off, and make the wagons shine in the sunlight, two coats of clear varnish. Finally, they would carefully paint in signwriting the name and address of the farmer. At the end of all this, there would stand a magnificent wagon, sturdy, wheeled, iron shod and shining, and fit to last a hundred years.

Charles (Clarky) Cooper junior had his smithy on the Radwinter Road, adjoining his father's yard and his cottage stood opposite the Baptist chapel, whose congregation sometimes objected to Clarky's 'strong wuds'. He rendered sterling services to the community. His work was extremely arduous and exacting, but wielding heavy hammers was a fine exercise and he revelled in his extraordinary strength and rippling muscles. He was often in demand by the wheelwrights to make the huge steel tyres for haywains and tumbrils.

There was scarcely an implement used in agriculture that Clarky did not have to make, repair or renew. Farm workers came with problems, for most of the labourers had to find their own tools. They asked for left-handed scythes, wider or narrower hoe blades to chop out weeds from wide or narrow drillings; men with big arms would demand longer scythe blades, and gamekeepers and poachers asked for long bladed curved spades to dig out rabbits and ferrets. He sharpened billhooks, scythes, sickles, axes, and every type of edged tool, often replacing the broken or split staves and stales. He made

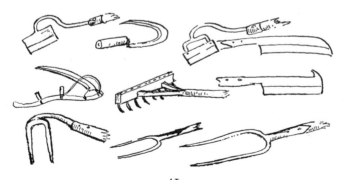

pitchforks and four-tined forks, plough-spuds, coulters, shears, drills and harrows; sometimes renewing the entire set of teeth on worn out harrows.

He would work merrily away, and the rapid ringing notes of hammer on anvil could be heard far down the village street as he laboured, sweaty and begrimed, singing or cursing according to his mood. It was entertaining as well as educational to watch him at work on one of his own chisels, to see the way he rapidly beat out the white-hot edge, held it in pincers and keenly watched the changing colours of the cooling metal. His brows rose and his eyes lit up, and suddenly he plunged the tool into the water tank. Throughout the hissing and steaming we could almost hear him counting to himself, then with a flourish he withdrew the chisel from the water and hurled it to the floor to cool off, without a glance in its direction. Sometimes he inserted the still hot edge of a cutting tool – but only for a fraction of a second – into a solution he kept in a wide-mouthed brown jar. Not once did he divulge what it was or why he used it.

To watch him busily attending his fire, throwing on nuggets of coal through small jets of water from a long-handled ladle, all the while manipulating his bellows with his left forearm, blowing cascades of sparks up the chimney, was a sight not easily forgotten. In desperate haste he withdrew white-hot metal from the furnace and pounded it with mammoth blows, making bigger sparks fly. Stripped to the waist, and wearing a hide apron, perspiration streamed down his magnificent torso, the rivulets showing white against the smoke and grime on his flesh.

As a farrier he had no equal. Shires, Suffolk Punches and Clydesdales stood stock still as he nailed heavy shoes on to their horny hooves. Clarky never had to renail a shoe that he had put on. A cloud of acrid smoke rose from the scorching horn as he moulded a hot shoe to the hoof preparatory to the final fixing. He cleaned but never trimmed the frogs, and blackened and polished each hoof until it shone. Horses leaving Clarky's forge seemed to hold their heads high and lift their hairy fores like ballet dancers, as if proud to show to the village their clean feet and bright new shoes. Children's ponies, the shepherd's hairy cob, and the elegant hunters of the gentry, were brought from miles around to the expert who knew them all. In spare moments he shaped new shoes to hang on the forge battens ready for use, and he always sang when making shoes for the shire horses. He meticulously measured strips of metal bar and marked each with a punched dot before cutting cleanly through it with sharp well-aimed blows on one of his well-tempered chisels; then, heating one end in the fire and at the right moment withdrawing it, he held it firmly with pincers over the anvil and beat it hurriedly, turning the pincers instinctively; and after heating and beating the other end we could see the familiar horseshoe shape. In next to no time he punched five holes through the white-hot metal, using a stiletto-pointed punch. One more quick heating in the furnace and with the ball-payne hammer he beat out the triangular toe-piece. A quick glance at it, and he flung the finished shoe aside, as if he had never been really interested in it.

Leaning on the doorpost of the smithy, hands thrust deep into the pockets of his hide apron, he would watch a pair of newly shod horses go clip-clopping down Radwinter Road, smile the kind of smile that meant nothing to anyone but himself, nod his head, and take a deep breath – perhaps it was a sigh – before turning to the murk and heat of the forge where many another task awaited him.

The smithy was the meeting place of the unemployed and the sick, who would congregate there, muffled in their old coats, some with only sacking thrown over their shoulders. They came for the comforting warmth of Clarky's fire in winter, and perhaps to admire a strength so different from theirs.

To keep essential horses on the highway in icy conditions he used his special frost nails in their shoes. 'Oi'm a-roughin' on 'em up, bor, jest to make sure they gets a bit o' pu'chase on the owd ice.'

He was our hero, idol and delight. He let us pump the bellows and gave us horseshoe nails for boring holes in conkers, and made steel runners for our homemade sledges and toboggans. But not a word dared we mention to parents about our visits. Clarky used to drink. Clarky used to swear something terrible. We all hoped we would grow up to swear and drink like him, and sport such great muscles.

When he broke out in bouts of heavy drinking the forge doors remained closed to horses and farmers alike for days, no matter how important and urgent. 'One bloody job at a toime, bor,' was his motto. But once off the drink he shunned it like the plague and worked like a Trojan.

For welding he had his special hammers, and knew their weight as well as he knew the heat of his forge. His joints were permanent, and he had his own 'fashionings', as he called them. 'I've got me mixtures,' he would say, and the recipes were known only to himself. There was not a householder who was not at some time or other beholden to him. Clarky mended pots and pans, sometimes for a copper, more often for nothing. Many of the old ones blessed his ingenuity for stopping draughts, for making latches for windows and doors, and footscrapers. And boys and girls crowded the forge for iron hoops and guiders to run and trundle to school. If we swore, or sang a snatch of song or hymn, he made them for nothing.

One of Clarky's pet sayings, uttered in his rough voice, was, 'It's a-gettin' wusser, Oi reckon. P'raps it's the different changes o' life we're a-passin' through!'

Ashdon's other blacksmith, aptly named Bill Smith and older than Clarky, was nothing like the finished craftsmen in the general work of the forge, but he had the reputation of shoeing horses quickly, some said better, but the shoes tended to work loose too soon and he would have to renail them for nothing. Bill's weather-boarded smithy was close to the centre of the village, and the main Ashdon-Saffron Walden road brushed his doorstep. He lived in a plastered and tiled roof cottage, a continuation of the old forge, all built so tightly to the side of the Bourne that the water actually lapped their foundations. The road between the smithy and the cottages opposite was less than 12 ft wide, a bottle-neck. Not that it mattered. Passing traffic consisted of horse-drawn carts and wagons and an occasional bicycle. Bill could fashion most of our everyday requirements moderately well, and his speciality was making garden hoes and rakes. Crippled and agonised by rupture, sometimes as deaf as a post, it was difficult to get him to understand details of any unusual requirement. He drew the descriptions on his whitewashed wall, and would make several attempts before finally succeeding in making the article to his customer's satisfaction. These attempts were attended by much loss of patience and bouts of swearing. He excelled at making hook and ride hinges, catches for farm gates, latches, hasps and staples, and his hoes and rakes, but apart from these he did not welcome orders for 'they bloody owd complifications'.

All the farmers obtained harness and hauling equipment from Levi Archer, harnessmaker and saddler on the Haverhill to Saffron Walden road, in the centre of the village. As boys we used to stand in front of that bay window, fascinated by the display of bright new harness, glittering brasses, and great saddles for the working horses. Levi and his assistant Albert Bassett made horse collars too, devoting infinite care to every detail of their construction. They had to be immensely strong to take the full brunt of the horses' enormous haulage power, and sufficiently padded to prevent rubbing. Indeed, all harness equipment for the shires had to be of fantastic strength. Only the finest leather was used, and many laminations went into the making of those tough yet pliable straps, which were all hand sewn with the waxed thread made by Levi and Albert themselves. They used a steel palm in their hands – like a thimble – to press the needle through the leather, working a double backstitch to secure it firmly, and the work was held between their knees in a wooden clamp while stitching progressed.

There were collars and saddles for lighter horses – the Belgian breed, the farmer's cob, and the shepherd's pony – more elegantly designed than those for the shires, and complete with traces, stirrup straps and girths. Richly ornamented bridles and blinkers, bits, halters, headstalls and nosebags, all were made in the saddler's workshop. And in the corner of the window stood a number of whips, which fitted into a socket on dog-carts and traps, and by them a huge umbrella, a familiar item when everybody travelled in open vehicles. When Levi and Albert were not making new harness, they repaired items for customers.

Levi was nearing eighty when Chris first remembers him, and he lived to be ninety. His birthday was 21 October, a date of great consequence to Levi, who used to state, 'I'm a lucky man, I were born on Trafalgar Day'. With his flowing white beard and steel-rimmed spectacles, he was a gentle and venerable-looking old man. During his long life he trained many apprentices, and Albert was the last of them.

Albert continued the business for some years after Levi died. He was a man of short stature and mild disposition, a clever and competent craftsman who was passionately fond of horses, and all his customers trusted him absolutely. He took his brother-in-law Harry Collier into his workshop to instruct him in harnessmaking at the time of the coming of the harvest binders. These first reaping machines had canvases studded with wooden slats, which used to get displaced or broken, and were brought to Albert to repair, and the great rick cloths, when damaged in a gale or wanting new cords, also came to him.

Mechanisation came in earnest after the 1918 Armistice. More and more farmers replaced their horses with tractors, so that less and less work came Albert's way. Eventually he had to close his shop and depend on casual jobs for a living. He was deeply upset. The shop is still there with its shining glass window, but it is no longer filled with bright harness and the smell of leather and polish. . . .

Chris remembers visiting Harry Smith, cobbler and shoe-maker, an old man before 1909 who lived in a little cottage at the foot of Church Hill, and worked in a small wooden hut just inside his gate. The cottage is still there, lath and plaster, with corrugated roof tiles, but the workshop has gone. Harry did not make shoes, despite his sign, but he was a skilled craftsman. One reason why Chris particularly remembers him is that his son Willie was the professional photographer of Ashdon. He used to tour the Ends on a tricycle with his tripod securely strapped behind him. His legs and shoulders were crippled after an accident and he had almost lost his voice, but strangely enough, while he could not speak above a whisper, he could laugh and sing as loudly as the best. He was a very good photographer, and some of his prints, though over sixty years old, are as clear today as when he printed them. Willie took many photographs, of Chris's family, weddings, fêtes and fires, but he left Ashdon in 1914 and only a few examples can be traced.

We had had two cobblers. After Harry Smith died, the other, Bob Matthews, served the whole parish from his premises in the heart of the village. Many called him 'Pablo Bob'; we never discovered why. He was very short and slight, and it was hard to guess his age. His dark close-set eyes were quite startling behind his steel-rimmed spectacles. Set up on the scrawniest of necks his head was small, and he sported a moustache like a Chinaman's, with the points clipped below his mouth. Bob moved in little jerks as he went about his work, his head moving like a wood-pigeon's. He rented a semi-detached house at the junction of Radwinter Road and the Bartlow-Saffron Walden road, at the foot of the Crown Hill. This house is now the village Post Office. His garden bordered the stream. A boundary wall used to run for about 30 ft at the back of the stream, enclosing an area in front of Bob's brick-built workshop which was built actually on the wall.

Bob made boots to measure for land workers when they

could afford a pair. Hobnailed boots were sold in both the village stores, but they had not the lasting qualities of Bob's handmade boots. He made them to last for several years, strong and completely waterproof, and before handing them over he would soak them in neat's-foot oil to make them soft and pliable. He made his own waxed thread for stitching, using a strong, double lockstitch, and the men who bespoke them knew well the advantages these stout boots held over the cheaper ones from the shops, as for days on end they were often over the ankles in mud and water in the fields. There were no rubber boots, but Wellingtons made of leather were to be bought, though the landworkers could not afford them, and were mainly worn by coachmen or riders. Bob often made leather leggings, buskins, for the farmers, with button side-fastenings and a leather strap. He stained boots and leggings with thick black ink, unless a customer required them 'left natural'.

Most of his work consisted of repairs, replacing a pair of clump soles, renewing hobnails, toe and heel tips, patching uppers, or reinforcing seams with new stitching. He was our only cobbler for a time, but even so there was not enough for him to do, and he was glad to turn his hand to casual farm work. At such times he would cobble in the evenings, and the lads of the village used to congregate in the shop and were a hindrance at all times. They baited the little man unmercifully and played practical jokes on him. It was no use fastening the door to keep them out, for then one of them would climb up the roof to place a slate over the stovepipe, and smoke him out. Sometimes Bob evicted them forcibly with flicks from a stock whip, and followed them into the road, but on return he often found his rivets spilt over the floor, his zinc bath tipped over and his lamp blown out.

Bob was a member of the four-man Fire Brigade, dubbed Fred Karno's brigade, which despite its comic opera appearance did some useful and praiseworthy work. At length age and financial straits forced him to pack up his lasts and go to

Radwinter to finish his days, where he had a married daughter. Bob Matthews was the last of Ashdon's practising village shoemakers, boy to man. After the 1914 war, my uncle William (Geezer) Ford received training as a cobbler. He had been badly wounded, but persevered and became a first-class cobbler, much to the daily delight of our village schoolgirls who blew him kisses and asked him to tell them stories, and always addressed him as 'Fordy dear'. 'What you got fer dinner terday then, Fordy dear?' The answer was almost always the same, 'Arf a brick an' no taters.'

Long ago an anonymous bard laid a curse on his village cobbler. I do not know whether he was an Ashdonian, but York Ketteridge knew the words and taught them to his youngest son, Chris. We have both tried to check the source, but without success.

> Damn the cobbler, and his awl
> Damn his hammer, wax and all;
> Damn his pinchers and his knife,
> Damn his half-starved kids and wife.
> Damn his hob-iron and his last,
> Damn the welts he don't make fast.
> Damn the heel-iron and the tips,
> Damn the brads atween his lips.
> Damn the hob-nails and the screws,
> Damn the lot – his boots and shoes.
> Damn his laces, leather thongs,
> Damn his fire-irons and his tongs.
> Damn his bench and smoky lamp,
> Damn his walls whully stained wi' damp.
> Damn his stove what stands askew,
> Damn his sooty chimbley, tew.
> Damn his wax-ends and his stitches,
> Damn his apron and his britches.
> Damn his rasp and leather file,
> Damn his jar of neat's-foot ile.
> Damn his inks and leather dyes,

Five miles from Bunkum

Damn his crafty, squinkin' eyes.
Damn his punch for eyelet holes,
Damn his uppers and his soles.
Damn his lump o' blackin' cake,
Damn the smudge he fare tew make.
Damn his ink-horn and his pen,
Damn his musky-smelling den.
Damn his lap-stone and his leather –
Damn and blast him altogether!

Damn the village cobbler ANON. (n.d.)

4
Windmill university

Above our old village there rises a hill
And right on its top is a tall wooden mill.
The sails, when the wind blows, go merrily round,
And there all the villagers' gleanings are ground.
The miller uprises full early each morn
And fills up the hoppers with ripe golden corn.
Then round goes the mill and grinds it with power
Till nothing remains but brown bran and white flour.

Blow, winds, blow.
That the mill may go,
Then the jolly miller will grind our corn.
Soon the baker will take it,
And into bread bake it,
And bring us new loaves
In the early morn.

Our village mill ANON. (n.d.)

Chris's family lived in one of the two miller's cottages close to
Ashdon Mill, or Bragg's Mill as it was often called. The mill
was only a couple of fields away from our own cottage at
Reuben's Corner and it stood as a landmark on the highest
point of the surrounding countryside. For two centuries it has
reared its sweeps and bulk against the skyline of Bartlow
Hamlet. Gaunt arms outstretched, standing into the wind, it
remains a symbol of the past, watching over the old parish.

Sixty years ago that mill pulsed with animation. Iron clad
farm tumbrils and wagons drawn by shire horses whose hooves
tore holes in the unmade road, hauled loads of grain up the old
Mill Lane which winds from the main highway. And when
the drovers arrived, Wuddy Smith, Barney Bland, Reuben
Ford and Walt Stalley, all farmhands from Place Farm and
Overhall Farm, Bragg the miller would be waiting for them;
his face, hair, arms and clothing smothered in the white dust

of his trade. Cottagers would walk from miles around with
their sacks of gleanings from the harvest fields to seek out
Braggy. Some farmers allowed the use of the barn floor to
thresh corn ears with a whirling stock fastened to the thresher's
stave by leather thongs – the flail. But farmers had no devices
for grinding corn. Billy Bragg would give his full attention to
those small sacks, reducing their contents to good flour, to be
taken home to cottage bakehouses.

On the top floor of the mill the grain trickled slowly into
chutes which fed it to the grindstones. From stones to hoppers
on the first floor sacks were filled with flour for local bakers,
or with meal for stockmen to feed to their herds. And all this
time Billy Bragg would be steeple-chasing stairs, floors,
hoppers, chutes and sacks as though his life depended on it,
which indeed it did.

There had been two mills in Ashdon. Some say the other one
decayed and sank into the heavy soil, for there is a circular patch
of dark green where it stood, but comedian Yorky had his own
theory.

'Knew it well. Used to stand close by to Springfields, jest
belọw owd Goldstone's on the Radwinter road. It were
simply a question of economy, bor. One on 'em jest had to
goo. There worn't enuff wind to drive the pair. Seein' as
Braggy's were the best an' studdiest, like, they pulled t'other
down.'

Sturdy it was, and Bragg's Mill is a testimonial to the mill-
wrights who built it. A post mill, its central post, probably the
trunk of a great oak, is supported by two mammoth beams
crossed in the centre under the base. Set on brick pillars, otherwise built entirely of timber, supporting the outer ends of the
cross beams, and being entirely clear of the ground, all the
timber work was unaffected by damp. A central steel dowel
passing through these timbers securely fixed the central post.
From the extremities of the beams four heavy oak timbers
support the central post, securely fixed just below the capital.
This rigid structure bears the whole weight of the mill.

Built on to the central column a turntable platform, the axis, turned the mill top according to the direction of the wind. On top of this, in contact with it, is another platform secured by a central dowel projecting into a second central post above, and on the upper portion of the turntable on which the first floor was framed. The outside of the mill, three floors in all, is supported by this platform.

The second central post supports a heavy beam transversely, and on this the second floor was built, the whole being immensely strong. It had need of strength, for there the millstones were housed. The wooden spindle attached to the sail sweeps pass through this chamber to the other side; and round the spindle, just inside the mill close to the sweeps, a wheel fitted with huge cogs engaged the upper millstone, while the lower stone remained static. At the other end a smaller cogged wheel operated the second set of millstones. A metal rod bored through the spindle connected outside with the great sweeps at one end, and to a chain pulley at the other. This device enabled the miller to set the canvas shutters to 'catch' or 'spill' the wind as required. Once set, the balance weights outside kept them in position.

Roofing the mill was the work of a real craftsman, who cut the timbers and put them in with hand tools. Under the arched roof which was covered like the outside walls with ship-lap boarding, with the additional protection of well-tarred canvas, the top floor housed three large wooden hoppers lined with zinc, constructed in the form of funnels with controlled exits. The third hopper stood above a great winnowing fan on the floor beneath, and held the meal for a time as it was ground before passing to the winnowing machine, which separated the bran and produced virgin flour. Bran and flour were then passed by separate chutes to the first floor, where the miller would be waiting to sack up.

Running just below a long wooden spindle, protected and strengthened by metal, was a fixed roller, each of its ends rotating in an eye. Operated by wind power, this spindle had long steel chains attached with S hooks at the ends on which the sacks were lowered and raised. Built one above the other, three hatchways with double doors closed automatically by their own weight as the sacks passed on the way to the top floor. Open hatches were hazardous because the top floor was 30 ft from the ground, so double doors were safety precautions. Sack lifting was controlled by a cord which transmitted wind power from the sweeps to the rotating spindle.

The surfaces of the millstones had to be periodically dressed by the millwright. Made of Millstone Grit, they were hard in the extreme, and once dressed lasted for years. Dressing involved recutting the series of diagonal grooves on the grinding faces.

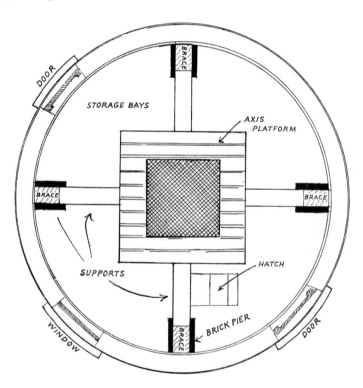

When the miller wished to stop the sweeps he would use his brake. This sturdy wooden rim, like those of wagon wheels, segmented and with movable joints fixed with hinges specially made by the smith, circled the spindle wheel. When the miller pulled the lever to its fullest extent the brake came into action, its joints clamping tightly round the wheel and stopping it.

The wind was never in complete control, irrespective of the force of a gale. The speed of the grinding stones could be regulated by governors, two heavy balls of lead connected to the undersides of the stones.

A flight of wide, oak steps led to the first floor, an oak stepladder to the second, and the top was reached by a cat ladder composed of pieces of wood nailed in rungs to the studwork leading to a slatted landing. Running down at an oblique angle from the first floor, and extending some feet beyond the steps

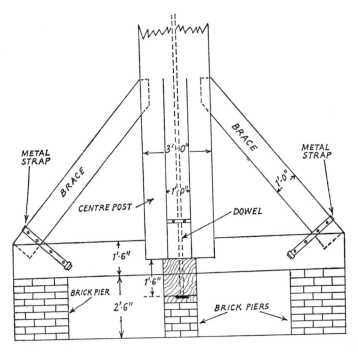

was the most important beam in the mill. On it were fixed iron levers by which the steps could be raised clear of the ground. This was essential when the mill top had to be turned to face the wind. On the outer extremity of this beam was a whipple-tree, an ash shaft with metal bands and chain links, to which the miller coupled his horse to pull the mill into position, 'inter-wind'. And if the brake was off, as soon as the horse began to pull, the agitation could be felt, and in the power of the wind the sails would quiver to life before beginning the slow, graceful movements.

Years before, all the timbers were wide open to the weather, but a red brick circular wall was built round the ground floor, with two doors and a glazed window. And in the 1920s an effort was made to restore the mill, but the first floor had begun to sag due to deterioration of the main timbers. Four massive posts were wedged beneath the floor to prevent the mill rotating. It was left in its old working position, its sweeps facing the direction of the prevailing wind. And there it slowly sheds its sails, a motionless sentinel.

It was Chris who first taught me to climb the chain and long mill ropes. I was scared of heights and he had to take me up on his back at the beginning, but in the end I managed to reach the huge cog wheels at the top. It was a good place to hide, no one ever thought of climbing chains to find a boy to go shopping or gleaning, and it was a good place to learn things from the new books Chris found for me. He would test me each night before we began to read in the candle-lit loft by the millstones, on Intelligence and Education. Memory training was the keynote; high on the list were Observation (aural and visual), Concatenation and Recollection. I was sworn on my honour to state loudly on waking, 'Every day, and in every way I am gradually getting better and better', and I did; we did not bother so much about the wireless programmes from 2LO Savoy Hill.

One day Chris told me to bring Leslie along. He unfolded his yardstick and measured us up, then wrote down the particulars. 'According to Old Moore's Almanack, in two weeks you should have new suits,' he said. And in two weeks he took us to Ashdon Halt to collect the parcel from the train. There they were, jackets and waistcoats and trousers, one for Leslie and one for me, our first new suits.

Harry Wright, the estate carpenter at Walton's Park, loved our 'university'. He often talked with us as he sat working on repairs to the windmill. Bits of his limed oak and fine workmanship are up in the top loft near the stilled, silent sweeps. Curled by the knife of his plane are oak shavings, crisp, yellower than oak yellow, with age, up there in the silence where the wind whistled. Oak was his favourite wood. With a twinkle of kindness in his eyes, he taught me how to plane the wood of the oak with jacks and smoothers, then dab it lightly with cotton wool dipped in linseed oil to bring out the grain, 'to see the beauty on it'. He taught us how to sharpen those oval pencils, 'chippy's carbons' to stiletto-like points with two-inch chisels without breaking the lead. His white apron pockets were always bristling with pencils and rulers. In his repairs to wagons, tumbrils, the splicing of their shafts, the making of ladders and other rough carpentry, Harry's work was never a millimetre out. In the finer work, the restoration of cottages or mansions, and the making of household goods, his work was perfection.

Barbara Wright knew how proud her father was to mend the mill sweeps.

> *The Croft,*
> *Church Lane,*
> *Little Abington,*
> *Cambs.*
>
> 30 May 1970

. . . I have a picture of Ashdon Mill taken in 1936. I can just remember my father repairing the sails. He took great pride in that work. He liked best of all to work in oak, then, he said, his work would outlast him.

He built this house (in 1948). It has oak doors inside and out and an oak staircase. I have an oak cased grandfather clock which he made, with his carving of Father Time on the front, and the bolt is a carved mouse running up the clock. There is an oak prayer desk in Little Abington Church which he made and carved.

When my sister Eileen and I were children he used to make us wooden dolls, diabolo tops and spinning tops on his lathe. He even made caravans.

He would be pleased to know that you have remembered what he told you about tools and wood, but he died in 1965. We put him to rest in an oak coffin, with oak furniture, and on his way he passed through the heavy oak churchyard gate which he had made and hung a few years previously.

Do not forget the men who used to make the wooden sheep-fold hurdles for our Mill Meadow. They do not use them now, but use a wide wire mesh which they call pig wire. It is as ugly as it sounds. It would be nice to see a picture of our mill in the book. I am sure all Reuben's Cornerites have a great affection for it.

Barbara Wright

Another place which gave scope for Chris's literary and artistic instincts was the former coachhouse of the Rose and Crown which was used as a shed for storing building materials. The walls were timbered, with virgin white plaster panels between the studwork, a temptation to any aspiring artist. A procession of lightning murals resulted, but they disappeared almost as soon as they were finished under York Ketteridge's distemper brush. There was however a poem respected by Chris's father and it remained on the wall for a long time. It baffled him but Chris was inordinately proud of it, modestly accepting praise from all and sundry. It was apparently written in Latin, a language which no one could unravel.

Sedito sali cum sedi anita longa me. Fors uper
abit o meta pio vel summamante. Foro midea miartis
ures o cantu caref orme? No tature nota bene jo
no dux nopes ome. O cari cantat allino tos uper
longae. O misere mi salis dum nodona mor tome.
O mari aggi molle cum anita mihite.

Chris was moved to explain it to me. No one else was in the secret. He had discovered it printed in *John O'London's Weekly*, among a bundle of papers from the Waifs and Strays Home. The translation is simple.

Said I to Sally, come, said I, and eat along of me.
For supper a bit of meat, a pie of veal, some ham and tea.
For O, my dear, my heart is yours, O, can't you care for me?
No tater, not a bean, Joe. No ducks, no peas, O me.
O care I can't at all, I know, to sup along of he.
O misery, my Sally's dumb, no dona[1] more to me.
O Mary, Aggie, Molly, come and eat of my high tea.

My more formal education took place at Ashdon County Elementary School, which was run by a headmaster, Mr Tuck, and three women teachers. It is quite an imposing building, standing high above the main road. Its main feature was the central gable with its clock turret. Few people had watches, so the whole village relied on it for checking their grandfather clocks. Workers in the fields could tell the time from the puffs of smoke and irregular whistle shrieks of the four trains a day on the single line track – two up, two down – from Audley End Junction to Bartlow. Or we could tell the time from shadow lengths of trees and hedges when the sun shone. But most people listened for the chimes of the school clock.

One large assembly room and two minor classrooms accommodated about one hundred mixed pupils. Boys and

[1] 'dona', slang for sweetheart.

girls had separate playgrounds, and porch entrances, but they sat together in class at long deal desks with slots for slates, uneven holes for inkwells, and irregular grooves for pens and slate pencils. Our seats were roughly planed deal planks on iron-footed legs. When we forgot not to slide on them slivers and splinters stuck into thighs and bottoms. I once had a splinter in my thigh for three weeks, and could hardly walk. My cousin Dorothy Whistler got it out after poulticing it at school with bread from my sandwiches bound round with a bit of a curtain. The splinter was an inch and a half long.

Infants progressed to Juniors in the two small classrooms; from beads, dolls and teddy bears to blotty rag-limp books. Then, on the way to the larger hall, 'Bill Tuck's big room', they would stay for perhaps two years with Mabel Eason to learn the three Rs, snippets of history based on dead and alive monarchs of the realm, and portions of geography taken mainly from the bright pink blotches on the map of the world, to which we used to sing Elgar's song about making them wider and mightier yet; and the pinkest and smallest called forth daily singing about ruling the waves and dispensing with slaves. We liked nature study and silent reading, but did not enthuse about the daily scripture lesson. Mr Tuck's room held Standards I to VII. Few children achieved the distinction of ex-VII, the highest grade, after which the school could provide no further facilities. Once a year qualifying pupils could study for an examination which, for girls, offered a place at the Friends' School, Saffron Walden, and for boys, King Edward Grammar School. The fees payable in addition to the scholar-ship were usually beyond the pockets of the few successful candidates, as was the case with Chris and me. Few indeed were those who went from Ashdon school to further educa-tion.

Although solemn prayers from the headmaster began each day's instruction, the school was a cheery place. After forming in single file in separate playgrounds, crocodiles of boys and girls awaited Mr Tuck's whistle blast, the signal for Mabel

Eason to play the entrance march on the tinny piano. We thumped down our hobnailed boots on the boards to keep time as we thundered into the big room with a song on our lips. The children were lively and intelligent and deserved a far better fate, for Ashdon was hardly worthwhile in terms of education. Although our teachers had the most valuable human qualities they were compelled to cram our minds with inconsequentials.

My parents were devout churchgoers and insisted that my brother, my sister and I went to Sunday school twice every Sunday. Besides this we were compelled to hear Matins and Evensong, for Leslie and I sang in the choir. At Sunday school we were given attendance books bristling with seraphs, harps and haloes, and bright biblical stamps with cherubic trumpeters blowing pink wind to put in the books – one for each punctual attendance and a faultless recital of the text and catechism. And when the days started to lengthen we looked forward to our annual reward, the Sunday school treat, held in the Rectory garden and the meadow opposite.

Swings swung from sturdy oaks. Under the monkey puzzle tree on the Rectory lawn trestle tables groaned with the weight of pyramids of bread and butter, scones, buns, tarts, bright wobbly jellies and pastel pink blancmanges. The biggest chair stood at one end, for the parson. Forms ranged alongside for teachers and pupils. At the foot of the table, near her orphans, sat Miss Whitehead, her rimless pince-nez on a long, black silk cord. Precedence at table was dictated by attendance at Sunday school, knowledge of catechisms and collects and ability to recite them. At three o'clock the Rectory family took their seats. Children were sepulchre silent. The parson raised his eyes and looked skywards . . . 'For what we are about to receive . . .' Rectory maids and other helpers handed round plates, poured tea in Coronation beakers from a gleaming copper urn and rapped snatchers across the knuckles. The table was cleared in next to no time, as if by a swarm of locusts. The parson looked again to the skies and said Grace. After a subdued communal 'Amen' there came an unexpected appreciation from ginger-headed chorister George Ford . . . 'We thank the Lord for what we've had. If we had some more we should be glad.'

We ran like the wind to the meadow where schoolmaster Tuck and others had whitewashed running tracks on the newly mown grass; to take part in the sporting events; perhaps to win a first prize, a whole silver threepenny 'joey' – for sack races, egg and spooners, three-legged, obstacle and the 100-yard sprint. Girls were gay with new hair ribbons, scarlet, blue, yellow and gold at the end of long plaits, as they swung on swings to a background of their own shrill laughter. 'Goo on, then. Push you harder. Hoigher, hoigher!'

Those not taking part in the athletics knocked tennis balls about with racquets supplied by the parson, there were no nets. A wooden contrivance precipitated a ball high in the air for a lone striker; several boys played 'rat in the drainpipe' in which a ball is dropped into a deeply inclined pipe and players try to strike it as it emerges. The usual cricket match between orphanage boys and village boys was in full swing. Girls played 'touch last' and 'ring-a-ring-a-roses', danced round the maypole and made the meadow merry with laughter. But the cheerful noises seemed to go down with the sun, when parents arrived to take home the young ones.

When night fell we had to rely on the rays of a candle lantern to light us home, for of course the village had no gas or street lights. Walking home in the Stygian darkness in the dead of winter, most of the lanes were overhung by trees and hedge-rows and were often ankle deep in mud. The lantern threw out shadows of a grotesque and frightening nature and the flame flickered as the wind whistled through the ventilator. When a heavy gust extinguished the light we children used to huddle close together to keep in touch, until with great relief we saw the friendly glow from a neighbour's cottage. Once when the lantern flew from Chris's hand and broke, he and

Bess had to save up a halfpenny a week to buy a new one for sixpence from Johnny Purkis.

Bicycle lamps went out with every big bump on the uneven roads or were readily extinguished by the slightest puff of wind. They gave out less light than the tail of a glow-worm, and we held the erroneous belief that a knob of lard added to the paraffin would reduce the tendency to smoke and improve the lighting. Acetylene cycle lamps with polished reflectors and magnifying lenses were a wonderful improvement. Twinkling dots of light warned pedestrians and other drivers that a vehicle of sorts was on the road, but usually it was the sagacity of the horses that brought the drivers safely home.

Indoors, shops, pubs and cottages all depended on oil lamps or tallow candles in tin candlesticks. The parish church was equipped with regal-looking, shining lamps, hung above the aisle but shedding little radiance. There was far more light from the stalls and booths of our village fairs and galas, for they were lit by naphthalene flares fixed to the gaily painted wooden framework.

At the mansion Chris first saw electric lighting served by a private generating plant. By the simple flick of a switch, without stench, smoke or splutter, there was light – strong light. Ordinary folk marvelled at its brightness and some went in fear of it. Old Jockey Smith described it as he saw it: 'That owd lected loight what they lug rownd on a cord!' He had seen Dixey the chauffeur using an extension light in the garage.

It was not until 1937 that electricity came to part of the village, and it was several years after the war before the service was extended. Even then sturdy individualists who had heard of the perils of electrocution declined on the grounds that 'If that owd oil lamp were good enough for me father, it be good enough for me!'

5

Around the farms

Wool was an important commodity of East Anglian farming from very early days, indeed it was responsible for the picturesque towns and villages built in timber, wattle and daub and with roofs thatched in reed or straw for the combers and weavers. Ewe's milk was considered superior to cow's milk. Old animals whose wool had deteriorated were killed for meat. In fine weather most of the sheep grazed on the downland, in winter they were kept in folds on fallow land and fed on what rough pasturage was available. As time went by they were fed on root crops, thanks to 'Turnip Townsend', and pasturage was cultivated as well as arable land, thus sheep improved and produced better wool and meat.

George Law (Owd Riley), a shortish man, but well set up, his rosy weatherbeaten face framed by Gladstonian whiskers, was shepherd to Alfred Hagger who farmed the 200-odd acres of Overhall Farm. My grandfather Reuben Ford, and Walt Stalley worked there for over fifty years. Many of the high hedgerows of Alfred's farm formed boundary lines between Essex and Cambridgeshire, and on these windswept Essex uplands Owd Riley tended his flock, sometimes 300 and more sheep and lambs. He was a familiar and much loved figure and it was reassuring to see him setting off in his cart, a scaled-down, much lighter version of the farm tumbril, his sturdy pony, which looked almost as old as Riley himself, hauling the laden cart along deeply rutted tracks. He would sit on the front of his cart as it swayed and creaked with the weight of foodstuffs, his shaggy dog trotting contentedly underneath with its nose just avoiding the empty galvanised pail hooked to the axle. Riley was the simplest of men and illiterate; he had done nothing in life except tend his flock, and this he did lovingly seven days a

Chris aged six, with
ousin Priscilla Warburton
anding), and sisters Kate
d Bessie

Father and sons: Duke,
win, Albert, Father, Jack,
rk, Chris

2*a*. Chris aged nineteen, with sister Annie

2*b*. Chris aged twenty-one, with crystal s

2*c*. Chris and Agnes, with
Dennis (right), Peter (left)
and Alan (1941)

. Spike (standing), with brother Leslie
909)

3b. Mays family group in 1914

. Susannah Reuben and Ford

4*a*. School group: Standards V, VI and ex-VII, with headmaster Mr Tuck (1920): Bess Ketteridge is in the back row, second from left: Spike and Les Mays are in the front, second and fifth from Mr Tuck

4*b*. Rev. T. H. Smi Baptist minister, 18 1920

5a. Bartlow Hills, from a nineteenth-century engraving

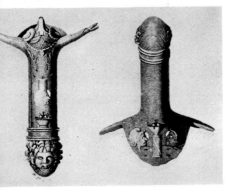

5b. Ornaments from the tombs

5c. Heading of a Court Roll of Ashdon Manor

6a. The pair of cottages at Reuben's Corner, built by Chris's forbears in the 1850s: the Mays family lived here (right), next door to Reuben Ford

6b. Walton's Park in 1908

6c. Bragg's Mill in working order (1910)

7a. Ashdon Fire Brigade in force at the Flower Show: Downham, Frost, Bob Matthews and Jim Freeman, being inspected by Major Pelly and Capt. Revill (1910)

7b. Opening the Rifle Club (1910): Mrs Thelwell, wife of Dr Thelwell of Saffron Walden, about to fire the opening shot, attended by Squire Pelly and the population of Ashdon

7c. Capt. Collins's beaters assembled at Bendysh Hall, Radwinter (about 1910): centre, with beard and game bag, Harry Freeman ('Jersey'); and far right, his elder son Jim Freeman, who went down in his ship the *Good Hope* during the 1914–18 war

8*a*. Wheelwright's yard

8*b*. The old forge

9a. 'The Clayes', which the Ketteridges practically rebuilt in 1929, adding another wing which cannot be seen here. One of the examples of their work in the village

9b. Arthur Grewes of Little Sampford, shepherd (1910)

10*a*. Joslin standing on his head when the agricultural strike was over (1914)

10*b*. Walter Marsh, hero of the strike, aged ninety (1971)

10*c*. 'General' Gordon disclaiming in Bonnett (1950)

11a. All Saints, Ashdon in 1910

11b. The army on manœuvres, 1912. Troops resting by the old bakery; the thatched cottages have since disappeared and a new red-brick Labour Hall now occupies the site. The photographer lived just over the grassy bank on the left of the picture

11c. After the storm (1913)

12a. Centre of the village: York Ketteridge senior repairing the plaster of Owd Riley's cottage. The bay window at the end of the thatched cottages is Levi Archer's harnessmaker's shop; on the right is part of Bill Smith's forge; in the background, Charles Eason's general store and Post Office; beyond, the sign of the Rose and Crown; and in the distance, old Matilda Fitch, wearing a black straw bonnet and shawl, approaches over Crown Hill (1910)

12b. The same row of cottages in 1967

week throughout each year without a holiday. His own rough hands had constructed the sheep yard at the rear of the farmhouse, a compound formed mainly of thatched hurdles. His lambing pens were more cosily roofed; ewes expected to lamb in December or January were put into separate chambers bedded with straw and well thatched, to provide shelter in bad weather and individual attention. From a flock of 300 a good half will lamb within a fortnight, and several within a few minutes of each other. During this important season Riley went home only to 'fetch a mite more vittels', when he was really ravenous. It is doubtful whether he ever spent Christmas at home with his wife and daughter during his 'precious time' as he called it. Most of his early lambs were born at the end of December, and he would divide Christmas time between the lambing pens and his four-wheeled van, drawn up close to hand in the nearest field. He would not take off his clothes for ten days and slept only in snatches in the hut, in which the tiny stove would often go out and if the cold did not wake him the first bleat from one of his charges would.

His new lambs were the first and last things in his life. He knew each ewe and lamb and could tell without a moment's hesitation their ages, where they were born, in what field or fold, at what time of the day or night, and the state of the weather at the time of birth. When he neared the fold they would put up a clamour of bleating for him; not a bleat was raised for anyone else. Fully weatherwise, Riley anticipated heavy snowfalls and would have his sheep in the sheep yard before the first flakes fell, and then set off with his old pony to distant fields to fetch back loads of turnips and other foodstuffs. He never complained.

It was common for farmers with no sheep to plant several acres with turnips, kohlrabis and other root crops which they let sheep farmers use for folding. This was beneficial to both; while grazing the turnips the sheep fertilised the land, which resulted in a bumper barley crop another year. Riley would take his flock to adjoining farmlands six to ten miles away, entailing daily journeys for several weeks, and leaving behind only the older ewes, six-toothed 'full mouthers'.

There was plenty of work for Riley, and it was good to watch him on the hillside as he meticulously set his fold, boring holes, driving in stakes and setting up hurdles. Now and again he gave an order to his dog, which would flash off to round up some straying lamb that had impulsively jumped the fold. But his voice was soft and kind as he unshackled a hurdle to bring it back, 'Come yew on home, m'dear . . . yew marn't carry on like that!'

His rosy face would light up in smiles as he watched his lambs at play. His wise old head nodded with approval as they skipped and frisked; and when he saw the contented wagging of tails as they drew sustenance from their mothers, his joy seemed boundless. Riley was a happy man in the only world he knew or understood. He was not much of a talker. He suffered considerably from rheumatism, which had gnarled and distorted his knuckles. He attributed his immunity from other forms of sickness to daily contact with sheep, and many believed that sheep warded off common maladies, supporting his oft-repeated statement . . . 'Jest yew walk rownd a flock o' ship once a day, bor, 'ould keep anybody in puffect health.'

John (Goody) Goodwin turned his team at the top of the Baulke, lifting his wooden plough handles and taking the weight on his brawny forearms. He realigned the tip of the plough-share for the return furrow. Whipped by a piercing east wind, sleet drubbed his leathery face and filled his eyes. He rubbed a horny hand across them and gathered the rope reins as with a sharp flick of the wrist, and an equally sharp, 'Gee there, Boxer . . . Up then, Dapper,' he set his team in motion down the long incline. He was aware of his three team mates advancing up the field to his left, burly Walter Stalley (Brassy) leading, followed at short intervals by Arthur 'Owd Fuller' Rule (meaning 'old fellow', the 'u' being sounded as in 'gull'), and Badger Barker. One foot in the furrow, one on the 'brew', they progressed with the lopsided gait of all horse ploughmen, heads bent away from the lashing wind, eyes looking ahead to ensure the furrows were straight.

Behind each plough the brown line of newly turned earth became streaked with white sleet. Faces were brick red and half-closed eyes streamed. As each man turned on the head-land he would start back without a pause, there was little comfort in dallying on this exposed hillside. But Goody took a bit of shelter from the trees by the side of the little brook, pausing to buffet his numbed hands. He did not see the stocky figure riding into the field on a rough-coated cob, but he whipped round quickly when he heard the voice, 'Now then, Goody. Don't stand about. I don't pay you for that. Git that plough a-gooin'. I want this turned over afore Christmas.' Goody gathered his reins, gave a hasty 'Up, there', to his team and turned towards the farmer. 'Thasser pity I carn't buff me bloody hands a minute to warm 'em!'

Amos (Mo) Hagger remained silent, waiting for the other ploughmen to arrive and turn their teams on the headland. He was the eldest of a family which almost monopolised the Ashdon farms. Amos farmed Hill Farm on the Rad-winter Road, Alfred the 200-odd acres of Overhall Farm at Stevington End, Thomas the hill fields of Rickett's Farm, while Joseph rented the arable acres of Great Bowsers. Of the whole family, Amos was the most exacting and the least liked.

Goody, the horsekeeper of Hill Farm, was paid 14s a week, and worked seven days a week – as horsekeeper he had to work on Sundays too. He left his cottage in Rock Lane at 4.30 a.m. to feed and groom the horses ready for the farmhands to take them to the fields at six o'clock. The farmhands worked a 60-hour week for 12s, and Mo made sure they never slackened. It was often still dark when the plough teams harnessed up, but the horses knew the old furrows, and the men could walk in them in darkness. They would continue until Goody pulled out his brassy pocket watch, and said, 'Come on, tergither, thass breakfast time.'

If dry kindling was available they would make a fire in the lee of a hedge and eat their breakfast by it, or with coat or sack slung over shoulders trudge backwards and forwards to keep the circulation going. Each man would consume the top of a cottage loaf and a mouthful of black, unsweetened tea from a bottle which clinked with slivers of ice. And in half an hour they would be glad and eager to resume ploughing, to keep warm.

At two o'clock trace hooks would be removed from the iron shackles of the whipple-trees and with chains looped up and hooked into the breeching harness the teams departed for the stables. The ploughmen would go home if they lived nearby, or to the shelter of cart sheds or barns, to eat their dinner – often the bottom of the loaf and the rest of the cold tea. But at three o'clock precisely Amos would be in the yard, to ensure that no one stayed longer than his allotted hour.

Goody, assisted by one of the ploughmen, rough-groomed his shires and Clydesdales with curry-combs and dandy brushes, then, after watering and feeding them, turned them out into the covered yards, or in fair weather they would thunder off, manes and tails flying, to the meadows.

Owd Fuller, with the old mare Gypsy between the shafts of a tumbril equipped with ladders, the latticed extension fore and aft to contain bigger loads of hay and straw, went off to the stackyard, accompanied by one of Goody's boys. There he hacked great hunks of hay and straw with a huge razor-sharp hay knife, leaving the cut clean and solid as the wall of a house, and soon the horse and cattle yards would be littered with clean straw, and the mangers filled with sweet hay.

Once a week they would go to the mangold-wurzel clamp. The golden root crops would be cleaned of earth and fibrous roots, pitched into the tumbril, then deposited into an annexe of the meal shed, where the stockman mixed 'cattle bait'. Here stood a massive slicing machine and various crushing machines to break down slabs of cotton and linseed cake. A huge circle of chaff was spread over the floor, on to which layers of the cattle cake and barley meal mixed with pollard or 'middlings' were heaped, followed by a good layer of sliced mangolds, and from time to time molasses, and the whole would be thoroughly mixed with shovels. When the mixing was finished the bait would be taken in wickerwork skeps to the various cribs and mangers.

When Alfred Hagger's flock was penned on one of Amos's fields, Owd Riley mixed his sheep bait in the annexe. Amos was a bachelor ('nobody wouldn't hev he') so the feeding of chickens and other poultry, usually the responsibility of the farmer's wife, fell to his housekeeper, who, with one of Goody's boys, collected the eggs after school hours. There were no laggards at Hill Farm, Amos saw to that.

Under constant supervision the remainder of the Baulke was ploughed, through which ran a raised footpath which Amos would have loved to plough up as well, but like Walton's Park Causeway (the Carsey) it was a public by-way. A corpse had been carried over it years before, and the by-laws had it that where a corpse could go the living could follow. The adjacent field, Wood Halls, was already green with autumn-sown wheat. Beans had been grown there the previous year and Amos, like most farmers, would never have thought of growing white straws twice in succession. Each year several acres would lie fallow, 'follow in it', and were rested, cleaned and restored. Many more acres were allocated to root crops, turnips, kohlrabis, mangolds and swedes. These were most valuable as sheep fodder, and many a bumper barley crop has been harvested behind a spring sowing and fertilisation by sheep droppings. For the special needs of the heavy farm horses, lucern, sanfoin and various clovers were grown as 'green meat' to help eke out the hay if the crop was sparse or below standard. Spring and winter oats and beans were their staple diet through the months of winter.

Root-growing was extensive in Essex during and after the

1914–18 war; turnips, swedes and kohlrabis for sheep, mangold-wurzels for horses and cattle, and sugar-beet for human consumption. Many varieties of potatoes were grown. Gathered in late autumn and early winter it was necessary to store them in bulk, in such a manner that severe winds, sleet and frost would not harm them. Farm buildings were seldom frost-proof or big enough, so most farmers resorted to clamping. Huge earth mounds stretched yards along the headlands, in the lee of thick hedges. Their construction entailed a deal of work. The labourer would plough the area to loosen top-soil, then shovel it, packing it at the sides, leaving a hollow of nine inches. Into this depression he piled thick straw and load upon load of root crops, in a conical-topped heap. This was covered with a thick straw thatch, always starting at the bottom and working upwards, leaving tufts at the top so that no moisture could seep through to the crops. Then the soil was shovelled back on the straw and packed down tightly, except on the ridge where, at intervals, breathing vents were left. Finally, a wide shallow gutter was dug round the base, and from it deeper channels were made to drain the storm water to ditches and land drains.

When roots were required the clamp would be opened away from the wind, and afterwards the straw was carefully replaced and packed down with soil and clods as before. Rats had to be watched for. They not only destroyed the roots but left holes in the clamp so that frost affected them. Potato clamps were seldom opened in winter, and then only when the need was pressing. It was always possible to store potatoes for winter use in a barn. In the spring women would be engaged to sort potatoes for seeding, cooking and pig fodder. It was seldom that a crop was spoilt by poor clamping.

When the winter was particularly severe, farmhands were employed under cover emptying stockyards of accumulated manure. This unpleasant and arduous task could last for weeks. Sometimes a hay-knife was used if the straw was long and over-clinging, but the dung was dug out with spring-tined forks with four prongs, carted to the fields and raked out in heaps on the headlands. If the weather was not too wet it would be laid in neat rows the length and breadth of the fields, steaming and stinking in the frosty air all winter. Mucking out was better than being 'stood orf', and the loss of 12s a week would mean near starvation. The only alternative for those thrown out of winter work was poaching. They used their native wit, and fed their families on game fowl, hares and rabbits, and some found a ready market for their bag with doctors and tradesmen.

Six months after harvest, seldom earlier, general farmwork was interrupted by the necessity to thresh standing corn ricks. Casual workers would be engaged. Peter (Rinchun) Richardson would be in his element, for he would be in sole charge of the long-funnelled, smoke-belching steam engine, for 'throshin'. Adept at repairing fences, gates and farm implements, Rinchun was never out of work however severe the winter. He always wore an engine driver's cap, and I personally believed he had driven express trains for the Great Eastern Railway; but Chris maintains that Peter never worked anywhere but on the Ashdon farms.

In the cathedral-like tithe barn above which doves loved and rooks cawed, Toby Woodley found winter work enough in the company of gnawing rats, in hand-threshing beans to feed horses and sheep. Beans were grown for meal, and were seeded by the bean barrow, a hopper-like box with a shutter, mounted on a plough. The seed shutter was activated by an iron wheel which turned in the furrow. As seed dropped it was covered with soil by the breast of the plough. The distance between rows was controlled by the simple method of shutting off the flow of seed for the required number of furrows, and God help the ploughman who was one furrow out – he would be the object of ridicule the moment the bean shoots appeared. Spacing was important. Room had to be left 'betwixt rows' for the passage of the shim. This implement for weeding was very like a horse plough except that it had no curved plough breast, but, instead, a series of cutting blades arranged diagonally like arrowheads, which slid under the weeds and chopped them low in their roots.

A muffled thud-thud-thud coming from the interior of a great barn in any farmyard in the winter months would distinguish the sound of threshing, and inside the huge doors, half open to let in light, a labourer stripped to shirt or vest would be wielding the flail. This was done on the floor, in the mow – the space before the door – and in the mid-sty, to the right and left of the mow, was stored corn, either loose or sheaved, until it was required for threshing.

The flail handle was usually of ash, a long handle called the 'stick' to which was attached with a leather-bound swivel the 'swingle', a length of blackthorn half the length of the stick. Blackthorn and, sometimes, yew were used because the wood is close-grained and tough, does not split or splinter and is ideal for drubbing the grain from the husks. Old hands plying the flail would keep up a continual rhythm for hours, 'swinging' the flail in either a circular or figure-of-eight motion. The grain accumulating on the floor was shovelled to one side with a huge shovel made of feather-light poplar wood, for sacking and removal to another barn for winnowing; and the empty crushed straw was thrown into the yard to be carted to the stockyards. Another pile of corn in the straw would be laid on the floor and the drubbing would begin over again. Every now and then the straw would be turned with the flail handle, then the monotonous thud-thud-thud would go on until that pile of straw was emptied and discarded outside.

It may not be realised by a layman that flailing, which was done by the Romans, is a job for an expert. Beans being threshed were possibly to be used for seed, and had to be done without splitting them. Long experience taught the thresher the exact weight to put behind his blows.

In the winnowing barn the grain was cleaned in a machine hand-operated by two men, and the name we had for it in Ashdon was the 'Dressing m'gig'. One man turned the handle which revolved the fan at high speed, and several sieves slid back and forth as the grain passed through them on the way to a chute which disgorged it on to the floor. The air from the fan ejected all dust and chaff through the open mouth in the front of the machine. The second man filled the hopper above the machine, and removed the clean grain from the floor. Beans were grown chiefly for animal feed, so a quantity would go to the miller to be ground to meal, and this was much used through the winter to supplement turnips in the absence of green meat.

The main cereals, wheat, barley and oats, were usually threshed mechanically, for which purpose at least one of the more prosperous farmers kept a set of machines driven by a portable steam-engine. These were hired out to small farmers provided they found their own teams of horses. A set consisted of the 'drum' for the threshing, an 'elevator' or pitcher to convey the empty straw as fast as it fell from the drum into its hopper, the chaff box which minced the straw into half-inch pieces, and, of course, the steam engine which powered all the machines by a driving belt from its whirling fly-wheel. The arrival of the threshing machines on any farm was undoubtedly exciting and found employment for several casual workers, who crowded round at the first rumour and certain signs. To herald the visit of the 'sheen' a heap of coal would appear by the rick to be threshed, plus a huge tank on wheels, filled with water. Then the pitcher would arrive, and the drum behind it, spaced to the extent of the leather belt which connected them in use. The panting horses next hauled the engine into position at the head of the line – a monster, even with its smoke stack folded back for safe transit. In motion it was a sight indeed which drew the small crowd of hamlet children round in rare excitement. The two men who manned the machine had to be hired with it, the engineman, who called himself the engineer, and the man who fed the drum. They used to arrive early to set about their preliminaries, the engineer wiping a piece of oily rag round his face, getting up steam, stoking his fire, and the blacker he became the more relaxed he was. His mate would set the drum in position and block the wheels, continually consulting the spirit-level built into the machine – an essential precaution as the sieves would not work if not exactly horizontal. The engineer paused to watch the gauges and dials above the fire box, and with a studied air cast his eye along the line of machines, connected now from pulley to pulley, shouting to his mate, 'Yow wanter goo more toward, Jim.' As a necessary adjustment was made, he would signal again, 'Yow got it now, sartny.' At last, everything being ready, he gave the starter a jerk, and with belches of black smoke and a white cloud of hissing, escaping steam the fly-wheel began to turn.

Towards noon the cornstack was reduced, the cart had made several journeys to the granary with sacks of grain, the sweating boy had carried many a bag of chaff to the stable loft, and the straw stack was growing. The mice which had retreated deeper into the stack now made frantic dashes for freedom, chased by boys and the farmer's fox-terrier, yapping excitedly as he darted, his tongue lolling. A mad dash, a scuffle and a squeak, and a rat met its death.

Everything was din, dust and excitement for the toilers, but for 'levenses' the farmer doled out generous tots of home brewed ale, kept for these special occasions when his men had to work continuously hard while the 'throshin' tackle were on hire'.

For a number of years these machines coped with threshing, until the traction engine, moving of its own volition and hauling all the machines at once, superseded them, and the need for horses passed. The old drum was in time replaced by a machine which blew the straw into a heap, and dispensed with the work of the pitcher and the two men who stacked the straw. This new method, though time saving, was wasteful, because the straw so treated was usually burnt as unfit for any use.

The farm really came to life in springtime. There was an urgency in the air, a new awakening, and every farmhand seemed glad to throw off the dreariness and apathy of winter. Goody and his mates would be toiling up and down the fields behind their teams, following sets of iron-toothed harrows, pulling down the peaks of furrows they had laboriously piled in the winter. Frost and snow had done their work, the soil was friable and tilthy, and harrowing soon reduced it to fine texture, ready for the spring corn sowing.

In the large open shed Rinchin prepared the Smythe drill. Goody and Badger were soon patrolling up and down the fields again, Badger in front, one hand on the steering equipment, the other holding the corded reins. Goody walked behind the drill, his eyes on the flow of corn being fed through segmented funnels to the coulters, which deposited the seed in the newly prepared soil, his drill spud at the ready to free any blocked coulter that halted the seed flow. Far in their wake, with a light harrow behind a pair of horses to cover the seed, trudged Owd Fuller. The same men, going over the same ground, year in, year out. The many miles they walked over the years can never be measured or appreciated, but they were a formidable test of their hobnailed clod-hoppers handmade by the village cobbler.

Seed corn drilling did not see the end of the spring activities. Land had to be prepared for root crops; ploughing and ridging, and muck spreading. Some land needed a top dressing of Guano – 'Compass' the labourers called it – and Brassy Stalley would do this by hand. Sacks of the fertiliser were dotted all over the fields for Brassy to fill and refill his 'cob', a capacious wooden basket slung before him at waist height. Using both hands, he would cast the powder to right and left as he strode along. He was so skilled in this broadcasting that not an inch of ground was missed. But 'sowin' a Compass' was a messy job, and the sower would reek of fertiliser for weeks. Stalley did not mind.

With spring sunshine and the warmer rain, weeds flourished more quickly than the crops and had to be checked by horse-drawn shim, or hoeing by hand. Thistles in cornfields had to be dealt with while the corn was still short, and the hand-hoers worked four or five abreast in their 'thistle choppin' '. Women were engaged to pull up docks by the roots, one of the worst back-breaking jobs, but they were glad enough to earn a few shillings. They would take them in voluminous aprons to the headlands, to be burnt by one of the men. Stone picking too was soul-destroying. They would fill tin buckets and empty the stones into heaps for eventual road making. Those who declined were quickly reminded by the farmer that they lived in tied cottages, and if they wished to remain housed the stones would have to be picked. Even so, the few coppers were much appreciated.

After the horse shim had cleared weeds between rows of sprouting mangolds, the women thinned them out, spaced to about six inches. Some farmers permitted the use of hoes, but most insisted on hand-singling, an ordeal of stooping and backache. If the ground was dry enough the women crawled along the rows, on knees padded with sacking. Once again they could not refuse.

76

Hay time, or 'haysel', began with bustle and commotion. After grass mowers had been bought and proved superior to mowing with scythes, everyone looked forward to using 'they new fashioned owd articles'. Goody perched himself in the iron seat of the whirring mower behind his horse team, Boxer and Dapper, and looked back with satisfaction at the orderly swathes of grass that lay in his wake. Badger followed on the second machine. Women followed with ash-wood rakes and light two-tined forks to turn the drying swathes, shaking them and piling the hay lightly in rows to mature. When the hay was harvested in the big wagons it was carefully stacked behind the farm, and for many days the newly built ricks steamed and shrank with heat. If the hay had been carted damp, a rick might well have to be pulled apart and restacked to prevent fire. Long iron rods would be thrust into it to determine whether the temperature had reached danger level, and these primitive thermometers saved many a crop.

Weeks later, when the stack had shrunk to its limit, Brassy would come with straw and thatching tools. With the aid of a lad to prepare the straw he would soon cover the sloping roof with a weather-tight thatch, raked, combed and neatly trimmed at eaves, verges and tops, a work of art from the hands of a master.

Now the meadows looked bare and pale, but new shoots grew rapidly, and animals yard-penned throughout the winter were driven into the cleared and growing pasture land. Shaggy and unkempt through the long confinement, they soon underwent a transformation, coats became sleek and shining, flanks filled out as they fed on nature's food.

By this time the barley fields were yellow, where carlacs (carlines) in full bloom raised their heads above the corn. Cutting off the flower heads was the only way to check these pestiferous weeds, and this was accomplished by the art of 'swanging'. A farmhand would move slowly through the cornfield swinging his long-handled sickle in wide arcs to sever the flower heads.

77

In July a golden tinge would be creeping down corn stalks as the ears ripened. Heads of barley and wheat already drooped with grain, and oats with the promise of a good crop. In August the whole farm bustled in preparation for harvest. Peter Richardson prepared wagons and carts. Everyone was agog with speculation about the weather, on what they would be asked to accept, 'to take for harvest'.

It was done as piece work, governed by the price the majority of farmers offered. If the farmhands managed to get an extra £7 for six weeks they were satisfied. Money above their normal weekly wages was earmarked to fit out their families with winter clothing.

Amos Hagger bought a new MacCormack binder, one of the first in the village, and Goody, who was sent to the Saffron Walden agent to learn how to use it, took pride in showing his mates how the sickle-shaped needle tied a knot in the hairy twine which bound up the sheaves, which were then ejected to fall in straight rows by a clanking, three-pronged fork. But until the headlands had been scythe-mown the new-fangled binder could not enter the cornfield to show off its tricks. Brassy Stalley was delighted . . . 'I don't like they owd sheens. Men allus come afore sheens in my reckonin'.' He lifted down his scythe, ran a horny thumb along its four-foot edge, hammered home a couple of weather-loosened wedges, and with his rub-stone began to sharpen the long blade. Amos had told him that Wood Halls was ready for reaping; that he and Arthur Rule would cut round ready for the binder. Alf Goodwin, one of Goody's sons, was to tie up for Brassy, and another boy for Arthur Rule.

Brassy cut a long, pliant wand from a hazel shrub which he bound to the heel of his scythe, bent it back into a graceful loop and secured it two feet up the shaft, forming a 'bail' to lay the cut corn into even swathes. Half a dozen scythe sweeps and the corn lay in a row ready for Alf to tie. Brassy soon showed him how to do this. Stooping, he gathered a handful of cut stalks, with a dexterous twist of the wrist split them into two, twisted the corn-heads together in a tie, laid this on the stubble and piled the cut corn over the tie; then, bringing up the free ends – those without ears – he twisted them together, made a circular knot and pushed the ends under the band, now tightly enclosing a sheaf of corn. Alf was shown once, and that was enough.

For two days the reapers scythe-cut the headlands, then Goody's new mechanical reaper and binder was drawn into position through the field gate, its road wheels removed, and the three horses reharnessed to the limber pole. Goody climbed proudly into the scarlet driving seat and took up the long cord reins. 'Gee, now . . . Boxer . . . Short . . . Dapper!' Bending their long-maned necks and digging in their hooves, the big horses took the strain and moved forward to bring the bright painted reaper into chattering life. Its sails dipped gracefully into the golden cornstalks in time with the horses' nodding heads, and bent them towards the triangular blades which cut them close to the ground. At intervals the triple-tined fork clanked and rose, after pushing out a neat twine-tied sheaf, then another and another, all the same size and lying in the same direction. Staring after the machine in wonder, Badger stammered out an unintentional prophecy, 'Well, bugger me! They 'on't want on'y three min to a farm afore long!' Amos's MacCormack was the talk of the village. Women came from other fields and even their homes to watch the 'new sheen' clearing swathes at each end of the cornfield, leaving in its wake tidy rows of tightly tied sheaves. Poofey Godfrey and his uncle Shunty Bill arrived next day as casuals, and began stacking the new type sheaves in shocks for drying. 'They're better to cop howd on, metty. All the same direction, all the same size.'

After sun and wind had dried the corn-shocks of oat and wheat heavy wagons rolled between the shocks, where Brassy and Badger, one on each side, began pitching sheaves to Owd Fuller, who was renowned for 'packin' a tidy load' – one that would remain on wagon or tumbril without roping. As the pair of shocks were cleared the boy horse-leader (often me) tugged the lead rope and yelled. 'Howd ye toight, gee, now!' The horse would move to the next shock. 'Whoah, there. Whoah!' As the wagon load left for the rick yard an empty was led in to be filled. The gathering of sheaves would continue with short pauses for 'elevenses' and 'fourses', when strong ale gushed from wicker-bound jars. But there was always a break of thirty to forty minutes for dinner, after women had walked across the stubbles carrying basins and plates wrapped in red kerchiefs, their heads wrapped in scarves, and knives and forks jutting from their apron pockets. Nosebags would be put on the field horses, and the men would retire to bank, ditch or hedge and open up the handkerchiefs.

'What you got in there, Brassy?'

'Rabbit pie, taters an' runner beans. An' by the look on it a mite o' apple tart. 'Spect you've got pheasant, seein' you were out larst night.'

'No, dussent bring it. Owd Amos might see. I've got bread an' cheese, a long walk an' a piss.'

Brassy was a bachelor until he died, but Granny Ford looked after him. The gathering of the sheaves would resume and continue until dimmit light, when the men could not see to work.

After carting, the horse-rake would be driven all over the field to rake up most of the cornstalks and ears. Bob Matthews, the cobbler, and other tradesmen who were not fully employed, would be taken on as casuals for raking and other odd tasks. Wives earned a few shillings by cocking the rakings into heaps ready for the final carting, usually the last chore before the field was declared 'open' for gleaning.

We invaded the golden stubbles without let or hindrance and gathered ears of corn that escaped the long narrow-set teeth of horse rakes.

Very early, after breakfast, we set off, the women's heads gay with coloured handkerchiefs, faded calico bonnets, men's red and white handkerchiefs with big knots in the corners, or men's caps with peaks pulled to the back. In a day of continual stooping it was important to shield the sun from the back of the neck. Over their homely clothing the women wore sack aprons, stitched to form voluminous kangaroo-like pouches. Some carried 'totty-bags' made of coarse linen and pouched like the aprons to hold the short heads of loose corn. This left hands free to glean and hold the long-stalked heads as they quickly grew into sizeable handfuls. Sometimes the 'long-'uns' were tied just below the heads with the gleaner's knot. We used to envy the old women's dexterity in tying this knot. It took us a long time to get the hang of it. Those who could not tie one, took scissors, cut off the ears and dropped them in totty-bags, or 'chob-pokes', as they call them in Suffolk.

As each bundle of ears was tied it was stacked. Each woman carried a capacious sack to the fields – often of her own manufacture from strong bed ticking – to hold the loose heads of corn from the totty-bag, which would be emptied many times before she left the field for home. It was a colourful sight, many stooping figures spread over the hillside, children interspersed amongst their elders to stop the 'shennanicans', all reaching to clutch corn ears, 'a-clakkin' an' a-peckin' loike owd hins!'

The gleaners were supervised by the elected Harvest Queen, whose job it was to see that no one started to glean until she had given the signal. Those who infringed would have their gleanings taken from them and scattered. 'Fair shares for all' was the motto.

At noon, the women would hurry home to cook for their menfolk in the fields, each with a bundle of gleanings on her head, while grandmothers and single women remained with the children, seated in the shade of hedgerow or tree to eat homemade bread and an apple or a pear. The back-breaking work would be resumed and continued without further rests until the Queen rang her bell at five o'clock or the school clock chimed. Bundles would be balanced on heads, sacks trailed, and the long procession left for home. Hands smarted and stung from wounds of sharp stubble, nettle stalks and other noxious weeds, sap from dandelions and docks, and ants, bees and wasps for good measure. Barley was always the cruellest, its spikes (avels) would penetrate clothing to infect and torment tender skins and would remain for weeks.

These discomforts were borne with fortitude. Only one thing appeared to worry the gleaners, it was the 'policeman' – one shock of barley or beans left standing in an unraked field where the gleaning would have produced a high yield. This was the 'hands off' sign to show that the farmer had selected that field to put out his pigs.

As soon as the ears had been threshed, the corn was taken to the miller, Old Braggy, to grind into wholesome flour for good bread. He would return barley leasings as meal. This was equally valuable to those who kept chickens or a pig. Nothing could compare with barley meal for pig fattening. Not many people owned a pig, but sometimes it was possible to buy a piglet cheaply, a 'cad' which fell below the 'porker' standard and which, if left in the litter, would be starved by its stronger fellows. Often they were knocked on the head by the farmer and the carcase thrown to the dung heaps, but if the farmer could be persuaded to sell one it became the family pet and was overfed by all.

After the wheat and oats the barley would be harvested. Being cut 'loose', it called for greater skill in loading, and the value of the new reaper was really appreciated. Neatly tied sheaves were easier to handle. Rickyards were quickly filled with new stacks, precision-built by Goody.

In the beanfields casual hands had been 'breaking beans', the operation of cutting with a bagging hook. Severed stalks were piled to moderate-sized shocks which the pitcher tossed on to the wagons. Usually the bean crop was the last to be gathered, and the women would gather the bean pods which had escaped the hooks and forks of breakers.

★   ★   ★

Around the farms

Why, listen yow – be quiet, bo' – the bell is tolling eight –
Why don't you mind what yow're abowt? We're allus kind
o' late!
    Now, Mary, get that mawther dressed – oh dear! How slow
you fare –
    There come a lot o' gleaners now – Maw', don't stand
gawkin there!

Now, Janie, yow get that 'ere coach an' put them pillows in –
Oh! won't I give it yow, my dear, if I do once begin!
    Get that 'ere bottle too – ah, yow may well stand there an'
sneer
    What will yer father say, d'ye think if we don't taakis beer?

Come, Willie! Jane, where is he gone? Goo yow an' fetch that
child;
If yow don't move them legs of yowr'n yowl maak me kind o'
riled.
    There, lock the door, an' lay the key behind that 'ere owd
plate,
    An' Jemmy, yow run on afore, an' ope the whatefield gate.

Well, here we be at last – oh dear! How fast my heart do beat!
Now, Jane, set yow by this 'ere coach, an' don't yow leave
yowr seat,
    Till that 'ere child's asleep; than bring yow that 'ere sack
    An' see if yow can't try today to kind o' bend yowr back!

Yow'll all wish when the winter come, an' yow ha'ent got no
bread,
That for all drawlin' about so, yowd harder wrought instead,
    For all yowr father arn must goo owd Skin'ems' rent to pay,
    An' Mister Last the shoemaker, so work yow hard, I pray.

Five miles from Bunkum

Dear me! There goo that bell ag'in – 'tis seven, I declare,
An' we don't 'pear to have got none; – the gleanin' now don't
fare
To be worth nothin'; but I think – as far as I can tell –
We'll try a coomb, somehow, to scratch, if we be live an' well.

Gleaning time in Suffolk 'QUILL' (n.d.)

6

Signs of the times

Here's a health unto our master,
The founder of the feast!
I wish, with all my heart and soul,
In heaven he may find rest.
I hope all things may prosper,
That ever he takes in hand;
For we are all his servants,
And drink at his command.
> Drink, boys, drink, and mind you do not spill,
> For if you do, you must drink two –
> It is your master's will.

Now our harvest is ended,
And supper is past,
Here's our mistress's good health,
In a good flowing glass!
She is a good woman,
She prepares us good cheer;
Come, all my brave boys,
And drink off your beer.
> Drink, my boys, drink till you come unto me;
> The longer we sit, my boys, the merrier
> Shall we be.

Horkey song ANON. (n.d.)

All the harvestmen keenly anticipated the taking of the Horkey Bough. When the last sheaf had been pitched to the last load the trace horse would be off-harnessed, a stout rope tied to his collar, and the free end looped over the bough of an oak. At a signal from the horsekeeper the horse would heave, and with a swishing and cracking the bough was torn from the trunk. This was hoisted to the top of the last load, and after a ritual drink of home brewed ale, one to the last sheaf, one to the Horkey Bough, the harvesters followed the load to the farm. There was never an organised Horkey for Hill Farm as there was for Place Farm and most others. Like all his family

Amos Hagger was a Nonconformist and a staunch supporter of Temperance; the copper in his brewhouse never discharged the duty for which it had been made, and his farmhands supplied their own home brewed ale during harvest time, in half-gallon kegs, complete with tap and spigot. They drank from the horn beakers handed down from father to son for generations, and it was a ritual that beakers were only used during harvest. Hill Farm's workers were not to be deprived of their own harvest celebration. They clubbed together to put on the important ceremony of feast and thanksgiving at the Fox Inn, where the landlord and the butcher next door contributed meat and ale, to add to dishes brought by wives for the big night. They usually drank a health to Amos, who perhaps did not deserve it.

For many years George (Toe-rag) Smith was the Lord of the Harvest and the man who always led the singing of hymns and ballads in the Bonnett Inn at the time of the Horkey festival. In the fields too his mellow tenor used to ring out across harvest stubbles in songs about ships and sailors, although he had never seen the sea. He was the horsekeeper at Ashdon Place Farm and lived in a tied cottage at the foot of

Overhall Lane with his daughter Laura. His constant chewing on oat straws to hide the horny wart on his lip which had embarrassed him for nigh on sixty years only called attention to it. Gipsies offered to buy it or wish it away, but George stuck to his chewing and his wart. Some of the younger hamlet children addressed him as Mr Toe-rag, not knowing that long before they were born a careless scythe-sweep had almost cut off his great toe. George staunched the blood and disinfected the wound with a dock leaf bound over with the tail of his flannel shirt. He then resumed his mowing of the headland barley in Woodshot and earned a name which he kept until he died.

He had a great love for and a profound knowledge of heavy draught horses, in sickness and in health. Farmers came for miles for his advice, diagnosis and treatment. Of the sixteen- to seventeen-hand shires, Clydesdales, Percherons and Suffolk Punches, he loved the Suffolks most and called them his roly-polies. Sometimes after grooming he would make them 'stand', and then he would show us and describe their points from poll to croup, saying how they had been bred from ancient strains, from countries remote, down all the years, for work on heavy fields, pulling and ploughing.

'They're a bit of a mixture, lad. Like some o' them varmints down the village. Same mares, but all kindser stallions, Brierley Turks, Darley Arabs an Godolphins. Mind ye, that's gooin' back hund'eds o' years, but not much more'n a hund'ed year the Suffolk farmers set out t'breed the roly-poly Punch. Can't be bet on heavy clay soil. Got short, tidy legs, an' can wuk all day with no more bait arter breakfast till off-collarin' at fower. Easy ter drive, not a mite o' vice, willin' as milk-maids.'

George had special horse brasses for his Punches, one for each side of the head-collars, and when he braided their manes and tails he used his special split-plait with the straw of rye.

I knew a great deal about his horses, for when I was ten I

was with them all day in the harvest fields. I had to lead them from one corn-shock to the next, and hollered louder than boys on other farms, 'Howd ye toight' and 'Whoah there', so the man on the wagon would not fall. Life was healthy in clear air over the sun-drenched stubbles, and I felt as fit and strong as Jack Dempsey, Joe Beckett, Georges Carpentier and those other boxers and athletes Tom Webster caricatured in the *Daily Mail*; for I was in secret training for the boxing championship of the World, and felt I was bound to win because I had three live punchbags – those bulging muscles over the near-fores of my three Suffolk Punches, Jockey, Boxer and Punch. I used to clench my fists, grit my teeth, get my full weight behind each knock-out blow, and lash out when sheaves were pitched to the loader at each corn-shock. But my hairy giants never once fell for the count. Sometimes – as if a gnat or midge-fly had landed – the muscles gave a bit of a twitch.

After I left school I drove those same horses, from the seats of hay-rakes, on foot behind drills, harrows, shims, rollers, and from the ridges of haywains and tumbrils. They always worked hard, never kicked or bit, and they were my friends. Now in the stables where I used to feed them and collar up and groom, there is emptiness, except for oil-stained tarpaulins to cover tractors.

Horkey was always celebrated on a Saturday night, with a holiday on the next Monday. With the harvest bonus many families went out for the day to Cambridge, Saffron Walden or Haverhill to buy new clothing for the winter. There was never enough money for luxuries but the trip to town was a treat in itself. They trudged to Bartlow Station in great excitement for the twelve-mile ride behind the puffing tank engine.

This marked the end of grain harvesting, but seed clover and roots had to be gathered before fertilising began again. The men would be out on the fields, spreading rich manure. Mangold-wurzels would be lifted later by casual labourers or

perhaps schoolboys. Soon the farm workers would be harness-
ing their plough teams to begin the eternal **trudging** back and
forth over the wide dark fields.

Stalley would be high on his ladders putting thick straw
thatch on the cornricks built by Goody. Each farmer counted
among his band of workers one specialist for building and
thatching hay and cornricks. It is an art that, like so many other
rural crafts, has disappeared. It required a high degree of skill.
The stacker estimated the yield and marked out the site for the
rick. Measures were taken to counteract possible seepage of
storm water and consideration had to be given to the presence
of trees and buildings and the prevailing wind before laying a
base of brushwood covered with rough bean straw, hedgerow
trimmings and rough herbage. Provided that reasonable
precautions were taken against the weather, rats and birds, the
farmers knew from long experience that the corn which was
stacked in ricks would mature and dry naturally, and that it
would improve during the time it was in the rick.

Sheaves were laid to form the proportions of the rick, sometimes circular, more often rectangular, and the remainder was
methodically built on top. The middle of the rick was kept
considerably higher than the outside, so that the sheaves
inclined down and prevented rain seeping in. This was every

bit as important and protective as the thatch. Ricks which had to stand for some time before being threshed were closely shaved with hay-knives, leaving a flat, wall-like surface which rats and birds found difficult to penetrate. Some farmers went to the extent of plastering the walls with lime mortar, two to three feet from the base, which not only kept out rats, but protected the corn from splashing from thatched eaves. The farmer of Newnham Hall set up a heavy metal grid upon which the cornrick was built. The supports had large mush-room-shaped heads and if the most acrobatic rat succeeded in climbing three feet of metal column, the concave head would have effectively barred its entry into the stack.

In 1912 our farmers were beleaguered by the organised land workers. From its headquarters in Fakenham, Norfolk, the Agricultural and Rural Workers' Union gained many men from Essex, who defended their right to belong to a trade union, and in the adjacent village of Helions Bumpstead where I was living at the time, a branch was formed in 1913. Forty-one farm workers joined, following the pattern set up in other parts of rural England. Standard wages were 13s for a full week of sixty hours, but when time was lost in winter and in wet weather, often as little as 6s to 7s a week. Out of this the men had to buy their own tools. By January 1914 membership had increased to eighty-two out of a total of 130 farm workers.

Employers were alarmed by the national surge to join a union, and in February four local farmers issued ultimatums. Two of them (Copy Farm and Helions Farm) gave employees notice to quit work and their homes, the tied cottages, unless they surrendered their union cards. The men refused, walked off the farms, and stated that they would not resume work until the farmers agreed to raise their wages by 2s a week. Thus fifty-odd men turned the farmers' lockout into a strike. Union officials tried to call a meeting to settle the dispute, but the farmers declined and the strike continued. A number of workers evicted from their homes were accommodated elsewhere with the help of fellow workers not living in tied cottages. A ballot was held in neighbouring villages in June 1914 and all the men voted to strike. 'Rough music' at midnight and dawn, ringing of bells, blowing of whistles, and thumping of tin cans, announced that the strike had started. About 400 men were defying the farmers. This was 95 per cent of the working force of Ashdon, Birdbrook, Helions Bumpstead, Ridgewell, Steeple Bumpstead and Sturmer. They were asking 16s a week for labourers, 18s to 20s for stockmen, 20s for horsekeepers; one half-day holiday a week and holidays for Christmas Day, Good Friday and Bank Holidays; overtime at 6d an hour, harvest rates at £8 for four weeks and 5s a day after four weeks; and for all tied cottages to be held on a three-month tenancy.

Non-union workers came out with the rest; one or two stockmen carried on in loyalty to their charges – and by virtue of police protection – but no one else returned to his work for the period of the strike. Union official James Coe, in charge of the strike, paid out the strike pay of 10s per week. The Dockers' Union paid £20 a week into the strike funds, and help came from other sections of the Labour Movement, which also sent speakers from London and local headquarters to Helions Bumpstead and Ashdon. A contingent of seventy policemen drawn from all over Essex was quartered in the club room of the Rose and Crown, Ashdon. Suffragettes came from London to harangue the crowds gathered on Crown Hill; open-air concerts were staged in the meadow behind the Fox Inn where to the accompaniment of a tinny piano and wheezy accordion the 'Red Flag' was sung time and time again, punctuated with frenzied wavings of red flags and loud cries of 'No surrender'. Tumult and commotion disturbed the peace of the village.

It was time for the hay harvest. The long green grass that had been cut was rotting in its swathes; the uncut grass seared and died where it grew. Still the farmers were stubborn; they would rather lose a precious hay crop than meet the workers' representatives, even though they were strongly recommended to do so by the Bishop of Chelmsford. The workers were obdurate. Eight men were arrested for taking a blackleg's pitchfork to prevent him harvesting hay; two were fined £2 with costs, the rest £1 with costs, and all elected to serve a month's imprisonment rather than allow the fines to be paid from union funds. They marched to Saffron Walden police station to give themselves up, escorted by 200 fellow labourers carrying hay rakes, forks and red flags, and singing the 'Red Flag'. The police superintendent – alarmed at the size of the demonstration – lined up his force in battle order, but when he learned its purpose he refused to put the men into prison; the seven who eventually served sentences were regarded as martyrs.

Demonstrations continued, daily mass meetings were held at which agitators exhorted the strikers to acts of violence. Hayricks were fired, wagons and tumbrils overturned, heavy agricultural implements placed across highways and by-ways to impede farmers and police, and not one farm gate in the parish remained unbroken. Animals broke more fences and strayed to feed on gardens and allotments. Untended arable land became foul with weeds; docks and thistles ran riot in cornfields, and what little harvest there was was gathered under police protection. More arrests were made and a number of Ashdon's strikers served sentences in the old gaol at Cambridge.

On 3 August 1914, the day before Britain declared war on Germany, the Farmers' Federation gave way to the strikers and agreed to reinstate them on a basic wage of 15s, keeping men at work in inclement weather, and paying harvestmen £8 for four weeks. The strikers regarded this as a resounding victory, but it was a long time before the land recovered. War soon swallowed all but old men, and the names of many of the strikers now adorn the war memorial.

★   ★   ★

On Saturday, 24 April 1971, writing in the *Cambridge Evening News*, Bruce Series paid a tribute to one of the strikers, our old friend Walter Marsh.

The day they took Walter Marsh to prison he became a hero. Scores of people carrying Union Jacks, banners and farm implements walked from surrounding villages to watch him and six other 'rebels' taken by train from Bartlow to Cambridge gaol. It was the climax to a revolt by about sixty farm workers in the village of Ashdon, against poverty-line wages being paid by many farmers in 1914. And it brought their plight to national attention.

Today in the churchyard at Ashdon, the village where he was born in 1881, Walter – the last survivor of those seven men – was buried alongside workers who supported him during the strike he helped lead nearly sixty years ago and the farmers he fought against. . . .

Walter and the other six men were taken before Saffron Walden magistrates for trespassing – going on to farm land to drive off volunteer labourers and the few farm workers in the village who did not join the strike. The seven trespassers refused to pay the fine imposed although the money was offered them by more wealthy supporters. Instead, they chose to go to gaol for fourteen days.

Walter was not worried about prison – his living conditions had hardened him to accept most privations . . .

He was one of twelve children. Their father earned 10s a week as a farm labourer, and when Walter went on to the land at the age of thirteen he earned 2s a week for a twelve-hour day. At sixteen he was earning 3s 6d a week. By 1914 he was earning a man's wages – around 12s – and the strike began. He and his colleagues wanted 16s but the farmers were not prepared to pay. He and other strike leaders tried to get support from other villages, but only Helions Bumpstead farm workers joined it. Others, tied to their employers by the subsistence-level pay, were afraid of losing their jobs.

In fact the Ashdon strikers were only able to carry on because of support from sympathisers who helped to finance them, some other unions and the Countess of Warwick, who had lived in the village.

Alderman Stanley Wilson of Saffron Walden, who remembers the strike as a boy and recalls seeing demonstrators marching, said yesterday: 'The farmers of those days, with one or two exceptions, were hard. They were mean and never paid properly until forced by law. The revolt was the turning point in the agricultural union movement – Walter and the others were heroes of the working class movement.'

★　　★　　★

Says the master to me, 'Is it true? I am told
Your name on the books of the Union's enrolled;
I can never allow that a workman of mine,
With wicked disturbers of peace should combine.

'I give you fair warning, mind what you're about,
I shall put my foot on it and trample it out;
On which side your bread's buttered, now sure you can see,
So decide now at once for the Union, or me.'

Says I to the master, 'It's perfectly true
That I am in the Union, and I'll stick to it too;
And if between Union and you I must choose,
I have plenty to win, and little to lose.

'For twenty years mostly my bread has been dry,
And to butter it now I shall certainly try;
And though I respect you, remember I'm free –
No master in England shall trample on me.'

94

Says the master to me, 'A word or two more;
We never have quarrelled on matters before;
If you stick to the Union, ere long, I'll be bound,
You will come and ask me for more wages all round.

'Now I cannot afford more than two bob a day
When I look at the taxes and rent that I pay,
And the crops are so injured by game, as you see,
If it is hard for you it's hard also for me.'

Says I to the master, 'I do not see how
Any need has arisen for quarrelling now,
And though likely enough we shall ask for more wage,
I can promise you we shall not get first in a rage.

'There is Mr Darlow, I vow and declare,
A draper and grocer in Huntingdonshire,
He sticks up for the labouring men, they all say
He has caused the farmers to raise the men's pay.

'There is Mr Taylor, so stout and so bold,
The head of the Labourer's Union I'm told,
He persuaded all the men to stick up for their rights,
And they say he's been giving the farmers the gripes.'

My master and I (Union song of the 1870s) ANON.

★   ★   ★

Some years before the 1914–18 war an experiment was conducted on the heavy farmland soil of Ashdon. Roderick
Charlton, fresh from college, conceived the notion of growing
fruit on his smallholding, Springfields, where for years only
cereals had been planted. Tall, thin and studious-looking, he
wore a surgical boot.

First he planted apple and plum trees, then between the
rows, strawberries, currants and gooseberries. While the hard
fruit was being established on trees, the planting and harvesting

of soft fruit provided employment for women and one ageing man known as 'Graggy', who lived in a Rock Lane cottage at the bottom of the holding. Graggy was a tower of strength. Between the sturdy old man of the soil and the frail young man of textbooks was a bond of real affection. Both worked through the hours of daylight, every day, and were rewarded with initial success. Bumper crops were sent off regularly to market. Had Roderick's health matched his zeal there is no doubt that his business would have expanded, but his health declined and he had to give up.

Over the hill at Sprigg's Farm, old John King Desborough who had watched activities with interest followed Rod Charlton's example. Acres of his farm which had previously grown corn were planted with saplings of apple, pear and plum, and between the standards, long rows of strawberries. A new industry was founded in our corn growing community.

A newcomer arrived at Springfields, Walter (Peggy) Lawrence returned from Australia where he and his wife had built a house with their own hands. Our local builders, Walter Williams & Sons, built them a new one to the same design, of which Starchy Williams said, 'Look more like an owd shed than a house!' But it was a home, for fine people. One living room, two bedrooms, it was warm and dry, and when things began to pick up a kitchen and another bedroom were added.

Peggy Lawrence had a wooden leg from which he derived his Ashdon nickname. A forthright character, full throttle of speech, he was held in high esteem and was renowned for cursing fearlessly at all and in all presences. His flaxen-haired son Wally, with the wide grin and Australian accent, helped his parents run the smallholding, which Peggy the practical christened Fruit Farm; part of it has now reverted to its original name, 'Eight Acres'. Peggy was justifiably proud of his fine strawberry fields and his orchard. It was a place of back-breaking industry, but of great beauty. Seven lofty elms

towered at the back, hawthorn practically surrounded it.
Stallentyne Hill bounded the right flank, and in springtime
a sea of apple blossom billowed to the left and down the
hill. His children seated on the five-barred gate greeted the
Thakes, Cornells and Downhams on the way to Goldstones
Farm for 'tater pickin' '. Later these women were employed by Peggy to reinforce the fruit pickers from the
village, Polly Webb, Beat Chapman, the Heards, and many
more.

Fruit farming is liable to disruption by the vagaries of
weather. When strawberries are in full bloom a late frost can
wreak havoc. Thus it was with Peggy. One May he had seen
tell-tale signs in the sky, and prayed all night. The rich dark
green leaves of his most promising crop were capped with
waxy golden-eyed blossom. But next morning, on his wife's
birthday, he found the frost; instead of blossoming life there
was dark, depressing death. His daughter had seen her father's
tears but once before, when she was four years old, when after an
accident Peggy was told his leg had gone. In the ruin of his
crop was disaster, the beginning of the end for this courageous
man. His 'Lawrence strain of Sir Joseph Paxton' had won him
high award, but now his occupation had gone, and he sold his
'Fruit Farm' – his 'Eight Acres'.

When the elder Desborough died his children John and Nell,
who kept house, carried on the good work. The fruit acreage
was vastly increased and Sprigg's Farm became famous for
huge Monarch plums, Early Rivers and Czars, which grew in
equal profusion to the fine black damsons and succulent
greengages. Strawberry production was intensified and provided employment for many. Although the greater part of the
farmland was still under the plough, fruit and cereal production were conducted concurrently and successfully until the
end of the war – with the help of Bill Mizen, whom Nell
married. Basil (Brisk) Fisher, one of the Desborough regulars,
took some responsibility from the ageing trio and stayed on
when the farm came under the management of Major Bill

Mallett, an ex-paratrooper. He further expanded the fruit growing area and commanded respect from his employees. To work at Sprigg's Farm today is a kind of horticultural status symbol besides a means of earning a living.

Eight Acres, or 'Peggy's owd place', changed hands several times. There was not the acreage or scope for expansion, but the trees which were planted by young Roderick Charlton still bear fruit in season.

At Bartlow Hamlet is a smallholding Chris knows intimately, for he lived on it for over thirty years before moving over the border into Suffolk. On this one-and-a-third acre holding a family of brothers and an aged father endeavoured for a few years to wrest a living from growing and selling fruit and vegetables. They were doomed to failure. The soil they tilled so long and arduously and so hopefully had been starved by the previous owners, and needed the treatment Roderick Charlton introduced at 'Peggy's place'. The Allen brothers were well known and respected. They worked hard and hawked their produce many miles round the district and far into adjoining parishes on a heavy two-wheeled barrow made for them by Starchy Williams. This barrow was well built and sturdy and was in excellent condition when Chris's brother-in-law Frank Ketteridge bought the holding from the brothers. Two years later Chris began a major reconstruction of the old thatched cottage.

Fruit pickers have filled the place of the gleaners of my childhood. They are gaily clad in colourful slacks and sweaters. The talk, badinage and laughter is heard from prettily lip-sticked mouths. Mineral water and steaming flasks of coffee have replaced bottles of cold tea. Old regulars like forewoman 'Girlie' Pettitt, 'Young Em' and Hilda, Mrs Pembroke, Nell Smith and Joyce Baker, perched happily on aluminium tripods as they lifted prime Cox's Orange Pippins from fine trees in the autumn sunshine. Tanley and Brian with their tractor-drawn sledges loaded the fruit boxes, while old 'Snack' collected the buckets of ripe fruit, and Brisk kept tally.

All owe their presence in those lovely orchards to two fine
men, the tall thin bookish pioneer, and Peggy ('that owd
Orstralian'), both crippled in body, but not in spirit.

7

Woods and woodmen

Will you take a sprig of hornbeam?
Will you try a twig of pine?
Or a beam of dusky cedar
That the ivy dare not twine?
  My larch is slim and winsome,
  There's blossom on the sloe;
Timber tell you, tell you timber,
How my trees do grow.

There are thorns on yonder mountain,
And an olive on the crag,
And I leave a knotted thicket
As a chamber for the stag;
  Lovely oak and spangled sycamore,
  The quince and mistletoe;
Willow will you, will you willow,
How the trees do grow.

Forester's song A. E. COPPARD (1878–1957)

Langley Wood lies mostly in Cambridgeshire, for its south-western fringe follows the boundary, although in places the wood invades the uplands of Essex. Castle Camps Endway, known for generations as 'Africa', nestles beneath its eastern fringe. We used to walk to it along the field paths from Bartlow Hamlet by way of Overhall Lane, or from Kate's Lane and Great Sandons Farm. Either way is pleasant.

Langley has many moods. In springtime oxlips paint the woodland floor with creamy blossoms and the air is filled with their scent. They are followed by wild hyacinths, wood violets, bluebells stretching as far as the eye can see, and here and there a purple orchis. In May and June just before the roses bloom the wild honeysuckle luxuriates almost to the treetops in many parts of the wood, the masses of delicate flowers alive with bees drawn by their intoxicating sweetness. In high

summer wild strawberries ripen invitingly in the sunlit clear-
ings, and there are ferns and milkmaids and ragged robins and
foxgloves. The wood is teeming with life and resounding with
birdsong. The shorter days of autumn bring fruits and berries,
an abundance of hazelnuts and acorns. Gold and bronze leaves
shower from the trees and as they settle into the ground there
is the mellow smell of their decay. In winter the woods are
stilled by the frozen mantle of snow, and few birds sing.

Foxes abound in Langley. The cubs can be seen playing in
the sunshine early in the morning, little furry bodies rolling
over and snarling and snapping at each other, but at a hint of
alarm, gone in a flash to the safety of their earth deep underground. At night the fox prowls the fields for sleeping partridges, roosting pheasants, hares, rabbits, rats, voles or any
other unwary creature. Only when other prey is scarce does he
raid the chicken roosts on a farm. Often he buries the carcase,
leaving a claw protruding above ground, and before leaving
he will befoul the spot as a deterrent to other predators. Sometimes when he raids a hen roost he will engage in an orgy of
slaughter, leaving his victims headless.

This brings the local hunt out in his pursuit, and Langley
Wood has often provided a backcloth to a gay scene of pink
coats, with a sprinkling of grey horses among the chestnut,
black and bay. The Newmarket and Thurlow hounds draw
the coverts and the rides echo to the short, sharp blasts of the
huntsman's horn.

A rough cart-track circumnavigates the entire wood and
once, long ago, this was enclosed by a barrier of wire netting
to keep rabbits out of the adjoining cornfields. As we left the
bright sunlight of the open fields we were aware of an exquisite coolness and the characteristic scent of the woodlands.
At first all sounds seemed muted, where the great trees, mostly
oaks, spread their umbrella tops to shut out the sky. Their
branches were alive with twittering small birds. The soft notes
of the wood pigeons were so restful that one could hardly
think of these birds as pests. In contrast came the chattering of

the magpies and the scolding notes of the jays who frequented the oak trees.

In autumn pheasants scratched around the roots in search of acorns, while red squirrels leapt from tree to tree collecting their winter food. The squirrel both hibernates and rears its young in its cosy drey, high in the branches of the upper terraces, so woven into the branches that it defies winter gales. The drey is most skilfully constructed of grasses, rushes and pliant twigs, with a lining of mosses, thistledown, and feathery fronds of the wild clematis, better known as Old Man's Beard. It is sometimes mistaken for the magpie's nest, for both squirrel and magpie nest high in some inaccessible tree; but in fact the magpie builds a grotesquely clumsy nest of twigs roughly piled together, an enormous pile with a kind of plat-form roof, the interior lined with mud, roots and grass. It lays six or seven eggs of a pale bluish-white, spotted with grey and greenish-brown. It is a thievish bird, and the gamekeeper's tree in Langley Wood used to be festooned with their black and white feathered carcases, in company with jackdaws, jays, stoats, weasels and screech owls.

Langley Wood is full of birds of all kinds, but the robin is always in evidence, with his plaintive little song, as he flutters down to search in leaf mould. The wren pauses in its tree-bole flittings for a tremendous burst of sound, its volume almost unbelievable for so tiny a throat, then darts away some distance before renewing its song. Its nest is so cleverly constructed from mosses and materials native to the wood that it is almost undetectable. The male bird builds a series of ball-like nests, each with a tiny entrance in the side, and waits for his mate to make her choice. She lines her chosen nest with feathers, thistledown, or any downy material, before laying her eggs, varying from six to nine or ten, mostly white with tiny spots of pale red. During the closest incubation period the male feeds his mate. Another small bird found there was the shy and gentle-seeming tree-creeper which clings tenaciously to the rough bark, searching the crevices for grubs and insects. Only its furtive movements give it away, for its camouflage blends perfectly with the tree trunks. Langley is a favourite haunt of the long-tailed tit, who weaves its oval-shaped nest covered in lichen into the branches of a shrub. Blue tits and great tits are there too, but the sweetest songster of all is of course the nightingale. Several pairs of these shy birds, whose melodious song fills the hours of darkness as well as the hours of daylight, come here to nest and rear their young. They can usually be heard in April during the nesting season, if the weather is warm, but once the eggs are hatched they stop singing.

Song thrushes and blackbirds are heard continually, and often the shrill piping of the missel-thrush, known in Suffolk as the stormcock because he sings mostly during showery un-settled weather. The chaffinch's plaintive call 'Wet! Wet!' is also supposed to denote approaching rain. Other finches are here, the greenfinch and the goldfinch with his crimson head and flashing gold bars across each wing, and the bullfinch with his strikingly gaudy breast. These are brightly plumaged birds, but the pride of place goes to the green woodpecker, a gorgeous creature with his metallic green coat, wings barred with various stripes and superb crimson head. His loud laugh-like call may be the first intimation that he is around, but he is not so easy to see. It is only with luck that one can catch a glimpse of him firmly attached by his toes to a decaying limb, his short stiff tail feathers buttressed against the trunk as he hammers away with his stiletto-pointed bill. The jaffle, or yaffle in Suffolk, feeds on grubs burrowed deeply in the decaying wood of tree tops. Two other species of woodpecker, smaller and of comparatively sober colouring, the greater spotted, and the lesser spotted woodpeckers, both inhabited our wood, but were seldom seen. Often we heard a noise like two boughs sawing together, which we knew to be the lesser spotted woodpecker, not much larger than a sparrow, drumming away high in the tree top. All woodpeckers nest in the hollow of a decaying tree, often enlarging the hole to accommodate their eggs, which are white and vary in number from four to seven.

The cuckoo came to the wood during May and June; so did the metallic feathered starling who added his chatter to the tree sparrow's, mimicking her notes so realistically as he perched near the nesting hole where his mate was incubating her eggs. Then there were the unmistakable notes of the chiff-chaff and the slurring song of the whitethroat. Below, as she disappeared through the ferns into the shallow woodland pool, sounded the hoarse c-u-r-r-r-k of the water-hen, her up-pointed white tail bobbing spasmodically above the brilliant green of her legs.

In the soft moist earth by the pond, a black velvet-coated mole inadvertently broke surface and in frantic scrabbling haste, disturbing the fallen leaves as his powerful shovel-like front claws tunnelled him back to his element, disappeared, and a moving ridge marked his progress beneath the mossy soil to an open spot, where in the middle of the pathway his tunnelling disturbed a patch of feathers. This is where the sparrow hawk had made a hasty meal. There too was the carcase of a rabbit, its hollow eye sockets revealing the work of magpies and the rats, who finished the remains of the kill of a stoat; by a terrible bite just behind the rabbit's ears the tiny brown sinuous-bodied stoat had sucked first blood.

Much lighter in colour than the stoat, the weasel is distinguished by its very pale underparts and its longer tail. It is a most inquisitive animal. When disturbed in its prowling it will streak like lightning to the nearest cover, but after a few moments it cannot resist the temptation of a quick peep, raising its head quite clear of cover. This was the keeper's opportunity; a sudden shot, and the weasel would be swinging in company with other predators on the crab-apple tree in the wood. Rats and woodmice, shrews and voles are the prey of stoats and weasels. Owls too find the woodland a happy hunting ground, but the gamekeeper waged war on the Little Owl, for these small dark-speckled birds will take young game birds at every opportunity.

The hedgehog too has a reputation for taking eggs from

pheasants, which nest upon the ground. This prickly coated animal remains in his hole at the root of a tree stump or in a deep rabbit burrow during the day, coming forth at night to forage for grubs, beetles and slugs. If any eggs come his way they make a welcome addition to his diet. Farmers used to claim that the hedgehog did infinite harm to their cows, by milking them as they lay resting in the pastures. Whenever this happened, the udder attacked was rendered useless for further milk production. Gipsies have always been fond of eating the flesh of hedgehogs, coated with a thick layer of clay and roasted in the embers of their 'yog' (camp fire). The rich golden fat exuding from these roasts was prized as a remedy against deafness and most ear troubles.

Langley is now a game reserve, and notice boards erected around one perimeter announce in bold letters TRESPASSERS WILL BE PROSECUTED.

In Chris's trade locally-grown wood was used for cottage building, furniture, and, of course, fences and tools. The heavy clay soil produced the finest oak in the land, oak that has built battleships and baronial halls. It is always in demand because of its beautiful grain and it is almost indestructible, except by fire. Few people today would connect the oak with the manufacture of boots and shoes, but in the early part of this century it was used for this purpose. The rough bark is rich in tannin, a chemical used in the process of tanning and dyeing to turn hides into leather.

In winter the woods echoed to the blows of the axe, the calls of fellers and the crashing of great trees, as cross-cut saws severed the trunks and brought them low. Felling was a seasonal occupation which lasted throughout the winter, but before felling an oak the woodman would wait until the last months to allow the sap to rise, as this helped in stripping the bark. At work in Langley and Home Woods, a family named Freeman were the local experts. 'Jersey' (Harry Freeman) added to his forestry skill the posts of verger, bell-ringer, sexton and grave digger. He had a son christened Harold, whom everyone called Thatcher, who could shin up corn and hayricks like a monkey. He climbed trees with even greater ease and was an asset to his father in the woods. It was usually Thatcher who tied a stout cord to the upper part of the bole to direct the fall of the tree.

Trees for felling were marked with scratches and cuts like complicated noughts and crosses. These forester's marks gave precise information about the time of felling and direction of the fall. If the tree stood in the depths of the wood the undergrowth would be cleared for a good distance to allow for the swing of heavy axes and the sweep of the saw. Careful note was taken of the balance of the branches to ensure that the tree did not fall the wrong way. Sometimes the heavier branches were lopped before felling started, and then Thatcher would shin up the tree and saw away with zest. The base of the bole was trimmed of small growth and a throat cut deep into the trunk on the side of the fall. Massive chips flew under the blows of the axes, finely tempered steel ringing, each cut clean and smooth. Then an incision was made with the saw which sang as the razor-sharp teeth bit into hard but sappy wood. The two sawyers had to crouch low as they worked to make their cut close to the ground. An iron wedge was driven hard and deep into the cut to take the weight off the saw-blade and prevent it nipping. As sawing progressed an apprentice drove the wedge further in with a beetle, and Jersey watched for the first sign of the fall. As the tall tree began to teeter, all hands were switched to the tug rope. A few more strokes on the wedge, and strong arms hauled away to creakings. Jersey sounded a stentorian call, 'TIMBER!' and quickly the wedge was dislodged, the saw snatched free, and the sawyers leapt out of danger. A good tug was sufficient to set up a cracking and swishing as the mighty oak crashed to the ground, to the shrieking of angry jays and rooks, and the splintering of stout branches that could be heard a mile or more away.

Pipper Free and Wuddy Smith then mounted the trunk to lop it of even the smallest twig, then sawed off the limbs into specified lengths for splitting with beetle and wedges. In 1921 my father John Mays and I both assisted this very hard work. The top wood was either collected for firewood, fashioned into faggots or besom brushes, or left to decay for years after. The peelers – casual workers or travellers – stripped the bark by levering it off in sheets with strange crow-bars, and very soon there were huge stacks of oak bark in the rides and drives, awaiting transportation to Bartlow Station, then to the tanneries at Cambridge, while the valuable trunk, looking pitiful in its limbless nudity, was drawn through Langley's glades by straining teams of Suffolk Punches to the sawmill at Bishop's Stortford.

Woods abound in East Anglia and in appearance there is nothing particularly significant about Norney Wood, some twenty-odd acres just over the Suffolk border. But it is different, for it is the gathering and roosting place for millions of starlings. This is no exaggeration. They arrive in great clouds from Norway and Sweden during the late autumn and winter, reinforced, it is thought, by migrant flocks from the Mediterranean and North Africa, where they descend in thousands on date palms and olive groves. But their numbers are puny compared with those that come to roost at Norney.

Each evening as the light fades the air is filled with wing threshings as flock after flock passes, wheeling and turning over the tree tops. First come the few pathfinders; then gradually their numbers increase. Many of the early arrivals settle on fields to feed, but seem to be waiting for the large flocks. Then, at some mysterious signal, they rise as one and join the approaching hosts. It is truly awe-inspiring to observe the black density of what seems like all the starlings in the world. Their wheeling evolutions are wonderful to behold, and this is only the beginning. At short intervals even larger flocks appear. They darken the sky and continue to arrive in a never-ending procession to roost in Norney. They have been coming for many years. Local people say the accumulated droppings have reached such a thickness that all the undergrowth of the wood has been destroyed. They usually sweep in before an east wind, at heights varying from 2,000 ft to 8,000 ft. Against an opposing west wind the birds travel at no more than 50 ft to 200 ft above ground.

Each morning after full light they can be seen leaving their roosting place. Old gamekeepers say that the air in Norney plantation is sour and that many good trees have been killed as well as the undergrowth. Local folk never go there to find out, but once seen the starling hosts are never forgotten.

8

Traps and guns

O Heavenly Father, bless us,
And keep us all alive;
There are ten of us for dinner,
And food for only five.

Grace JOSEPH ARCH (1826–1919)

Poaching was always a criminal offence. Anyone caught in the act was severely punished. Many a farm labourer practised it for the sake of his famished family and developed the crime into an art. Eight, ten or fifteen children was not unusual in families. There were many unemployed and no unemployment benefit. Even men with steady jobs had to scheme to provide meat meals; the others existed on threshing, harvesting or other seasonal work. They were the nucleus of the poaching gang, who did not regard poaching as stealing. For what man would see his child go hungry to bed when rabbits and hares abounded?

Nightly they taxed the vigilance of gamekeepers, two of whom were my uncles Jasper Miller and Baldy Rodwell. All kinds of ingenious methods were used to outwit the protectors of game and vermin. It was mainly the solitary poacher who was caught and fined. If he could not pay, as was usually the case, the alternative was imprisonment – one month for snaring one rabbit. The gangs worked out their campaigns with all the care of Commandos planning a night raid. Two or three men with shotguns would create a diversion by firing outside one wood, which brought gamekeepers and a policeman to the spot; in the meantime, a mile or so away, the raid itself would take place. At the sound of fresh shots the gamekeepers would hurry to the second place; but they always arrived too late, as the poachers had worked silently and were by that time far away with a good bag of pheasant. The first firers then made their foray deep into the first wood while the gamekeepers were searching elsewhere. They slung their guns over their shoulders and from deep pockets took out catapults and lanterns. Some used bows and arrows, for to the silent and the swift came success.

Old hands knew how to lure pheasant and partridge into their cottage gardens and allotments. Most of their methods remained secrets. All were versed in the art of making snares, setting them with the wire noose at the right height for hare or rabbit, and staking them correctly for quick recovery. Nets of strong twine, used only on dark nights, needed two men and long lurcher dogs. The net was fastened to one gatepost, stretched across the open gateway and the other end held by a man crouching near the opposite post. The second man walked towards him, the dogs ranging in wide circles as they were trained to do. Hares would be flushed from their forms and made for the gateway, to be trapped in the net and lifted out by their long ears to instant death by the heel of a poacher's palm. They sold well. No questions were asked.

A drag net was used over stubble to catch partridges, but to counter this the gamekeepers cut blackthorn and white-thorn and planted them all over the fields as soon as farmers had cleared their stubbles.

Ferrets were put into rabbit holes which honeycombed a dry bank, most of them temporarily blocked, leaving one or two bolt holes to which were fixed poacher's nets into which rabbits shot like lightning when confronted with the ferret. Usually, by the time daylight was shining in the east, the bag would be heavy, but the gang never pressed their luck too far. Butchers gave sixpence a head for rabbits.

Old Allen had a pheasant dinner whenever he wanted one. He did not need much in the way of equipment. One reel of black cotton, one tin wash basin, one piece of stick 8 in long, and a handful of wheat soaked in rhubarb wine. Pheasants were partial to such wheat. Allen used to prop the basin upside down on the stick to which he had attached one end of a length of cotton. He then walked backwards to his toolshed, unwinding the cotton and trailing it over the grass, and hung the reel on a nail. From the hedge overlooking Overhall Lane he put down a trail of soaked wheat, leading to the basin, and piled up more grain. He would then retire to his shed and wait for the reel to knock the window pane. A walk of twenty yards, a lift of the basin, and there, with luck, was a cock bird.

Mossy Harris, a hay tyer and thatcher when he worked, was one of the best known poachers in Ashdon, partly because he was a lone wolf and was frequently caught. He did not poach from necessity. He was a bachelor and could make a living by his trade, but it appealed to his sense of adventure. He lived with his old parents and caused them much heartache. He rode a penny-farthing to work, often enough hopelessly drunk, but he never fell off. His carelessness in poaching made him a familiar figure in the magistrate's court, and it was said that the authorities anticipated his appearance with some degree of accuracy. Mossy used to boast that Cambridge gaol was his second home. The same cell was always ready for him.

Another offender of gamekeepers was 'Snooky', a man of indifferent health who lived by poaching and spent many periods in prison. He served in the army throughout the 1914–18 war, which wrecked his health, and died soon after his demobilisation. Ashdon gave him full military honours

when they buried him, mainly because he was a poacher. He was afterwards remembered as a war hero.

Farm labourer and jack-of-all-trades Bill Walls had an aggressive exterior, but unless provoked he was the mildest of men. Tall, rangy, with piercing eyes and bristling whiskers, he strode across the fields as if he wore seven-league boots; he seemed to be battling against some invisible force which impeded his progress when he wished to hurry. Bill had three unexplained nicknames, 'Quim', 'The Old File' and 'The Philosopher'.

Chris first met him at the age of thirteen when he started work with his father York Ketteridge, who was making repairs to the mansion, Walton's Park. Because Bill's strength was Herculean, York had taken him on as a labourer. Bill took Chris, who was small for his age, under his kindly wing, showed him a trick or two about the building trade, and a great many more about the problems of life. His rapid speech was made unusually attractive and mellow by an impediment. He could not sound his Rs. 'Owd Quim,' said the villagers, 'can talk the hind leg orf a donkey.'

It was not until after the war that Chris got to know the deeper side of Bill. After making a number of crystal sets, Chris had just built a one-valve wireless receiver. There were not a dozen cat's-whisker wirelesses in the village, and organised broadcasting had just begun. One evening Bill came to Mill Cottage to see York and was immediately interested in Chris's new set. When Chris placed a pair of headphones over his ears, his face lit up as he listened enthralled to a piano recital by Paderewski. For once speech failed him. Often afterwards he would come to listen to the wireless and talk about music, and one day he talked about himself.

'Well, I went to penny school until I was eleven. Left to start work on the cruellest job any boy could do. Watering the spade of old Dan Unwin, land-ditching on the Fan in the middle of winter. The east wind blew right through me. Yes, brought us up hard in those days. I've often thought about it, like I did in after years when I left home. Well, they had nothing on the farm but bloody hard work, seven bob for a sixty-hour week, every day and in all weathers. I was as strong then as I am today, and reckoned I was as good as any man and ought to have a better chance in life. I had a relation at Greenwich. Told me I could get a job in a gas hole there. One morning I put on my best jacket, said nothing to a soul and just buggered off. Took me two days. Walked all the way. Slept one night under a haystack t'other side of Stortford. Got the job and lodged with my relation.

'Worn't no wuss orf, nor yet much better. The work was hard, but no harder than the land. More money, but more to spend. Never regretted that because I got hold of plenty of good books. That's where I got my mite of education. It was the finest thing I ever did when I learned to read at penny school. Through my books I learned as much as they teach in some colleges, and I was working hard during the day as well. Found out about history, geography, English, music and drama; read the best poets and writers and was able to go to concerts – not those tuppence-ha'porths we have here, real concerts with great orchestras playing Bach, Wagner and Beethoven. Then when I left I never thought I should hear such music again, but I was wrong.'

He pointed to the wireless set.

'I've been back a long time. You see, Chris, it was my old bellows. I couldn't stick the stink of gas any longer. I was taken ill and the quack told me if I wished to recover I should get back to the fresh air of the country. So I came back to Ashdon where I was pupped. Didn't go back to the land right away, got a job with Mr Gibbs, planting trees on Bartlow Estate for the Reverend Brocklebank. Pretty good job, got a shilling more than farmers were paying. Twelve bob for a sixty-hour week, nearly twice as much as when I started . . . There they are, look at 'em!'

And there they were, in spinneys, copses, thickets, rookeries and hedges, all over the estate. Some years later old Bill was back on a farm, working as driver's mate to Peter Richardson who was in charge of the black-smoke spouting traction engine and some threshing tackle, which had begun to ply between the parish farms. Bill had a hankering after machinery. Asked what he would do if he could begin life anew, he pulled himself to his six feet-plus, his ageing eyes flashing.

'Like the bloody fool I am, I should do as I did in the past. But I'd like to see more education for us country folk. Something's got to be done now mechanisation has took on. Anyhow, we can't expect to be more than God intended. I've been through the bloody mill, but seen plenty worse off, and I've always been able to enjoy a pint and a bit o' baccy. The man with the least is the happiest in the long run. Less to worry about. There's no woman or childer to mourn me, Chris. I'm the happiest bugger alive!'

In the autumn of 1919 Christopher Ketteridge and a score of other tradesmen and farmhands assembled in the large kitchen yard of Walton's Park for a day's field driving to the guns of Major Tansley Luddington's shooting party. Henry Rodwell, the major's gamekeeper (later to become my uncle by marrying my Aunt Frances), was there to brief them about the route. At the time I was boot-boy, though still at school. Rodwell was well past his prime, with only one hair on his head, and neither lash nor brow – a state which had gained him the Ashdon nickname, 'One hair and a nit. He used strong language on all occasions, with or without provocation, even to his gentlemanly employer who never took exception. Rodwell had been with Major Luddington for many years before they came to Ashdon. It was said he lost his hair and gained his strong tongue after being knocked senseless by poachers and left for dead. He always accompanied the squire on tours of his coverts, seated beside him in the high dog-cart. Once Chris was digging the garden when he heard loud voices and looking up he saw the dog-cart emerging from Mill Meadow. The major, who was driving, took the turning into

Mill Lane a bit too tightly. The hub of a wheel fouled the gatepost and the dog-cart rocked dangerously. Rodwell clutched his hat with one hand and the flat mudguard with the other. 'God blast ye,' he yelled, glaring at his employer as if he were a serf, 'You'll hev the bluddy cart over, we an' all. You wanter look where your a-gooin', or goo where you're a-bluddy lookin'!' The major merely chuckled and carried on.

Despite his forceful address Rodwell was most deeply attached to Major Luddington. It was something akin to hero worship.

'Talk about shoot! Why he can knock a flea's eye out clean as a bluddy whistle, even though he do shoot back'ards, like!'

Luddington always used a specially made gun with a curved stock, for he was right-handed and fired from the right shoulder, but always sighted with his left eye. He was a crack shot and a thorough sportsman. When birds were being driven he would never fire forward in the direction of the beaters, but would wait until the covey passed overhead. Then he would pivot round and in rapid succession pick off the two outside birds, a left, and then a right. He never failed to bag those two, however windy or difficult the conditions, and Rodwell was always elated. One would think he had shot the birds himself. The major was usually soft of speech and gentle of manner; but on the last shoot but one of that season, when the order of shoot was 'cock birds only', he actually shouted.

We were beating the coverts of Home Wood from which we were about to emerge, having flushed the birds from cover to the long line of guns. Chris was close to Major Luddington when a bird screeched and flew, and from Rodwell came a roar, 'HEN PHEASANT!'

A shot rang out and the bird almost disintegrated. Like a tiger the major turned on the marksman. 'Are you bloody-well blind and deaf into the bargain?'

Hen birds were needed to hatch and rear the next broods. It

was indefensible to shoot them at the tail of the season. The culprit had his gun cancelled and never shot at Walton's again.

The beaters were strung out in line across the stubble on those tranquil days of autumn when the ground was firm and dry, and though we walked a good dozen miles a day driving before us the hares and partridges we were never tired. But later in the season, after golden stubble had been transmuted to brown by the plough, it was a different proposition. Each foot collected a heavy ball of mud, and one had to kick violently to dislodge it. Each new pace was an effort of lifting, and leg muscles burned and ached, taking the fun out of our 'big day'.

'Owd Nickett' who lived at Camps End regularly attended these brushing parties, as we called them. He was walking next to Chris as they were closing on Langley Wood, and they were very mud-bound at the time. A covey of partridge broke cover and rose swiftly on the wind. Nickett croaked a tooth-less laugh, 'Bloody fools, ain't we, Chris, bor? A-walkin' arter things wot floy!' This was the joke running through the village, which made everybody laugh, but I do not know who started it. A hare leapt from its form under Nickett's mud-clogged feet and streaked to its doom. A gun crashed at the edge of the wood. The hare somersaulted high into bush-growth, then fell. 'There, there, now!' said Nickett, 'Ef that silly bugger hanter got up an' laid still, that'd still be a-runnin', 'ouldn't it?'

Like his three brothers, Pipper, Pie and Ninn, he was a dry old stick, and his company enlivened many a leg-aching slog in the miry fields. Most of all we liked to beat the woods, especially in dry weather. We tried to keep in sight of our friends on right and left, and were helped to a large extent by obeying Rodwell's barrack-square orders as we entered the tangled undergrowth of the untrimmed glades.

'Rattle yar owd sticks, you lazy buggers. Keep a-hollerin' well, an' a-bellerin' well, an' make plenty o' row!'

This was right up our street, or wood, and we obliged with

all the din we could produce, which was punctuated by calls to the guns, 'Mark over', 'Cock over', 'Woodcock forrard', and intermittent shrillings of the keeper's whistle as he signalled the species of bird to the waiting guns. It was a process of continual dodging and stooping to avoid low branches, and frequent pausing to extricate clothing from sprawling bramble-growth; but Rodwell would be on the lookout for those who became entangled.

'Come you on, tergither. Keep up oo the others, blast an' bugger ye!'

In the woodlands at the beginning of the shooting season there was always that wonderful autumn tang, which is intensified after rain. But beating the woods in wet weather was most unpleasant. We not only got soaked to the skin, but we also became filthy from the slimy undergrowth. Even so, it fired our young imagination. We had become hunters, adventurers, the Stanleys and Livingstones of the deepest and densest jungles of non-Equatorial East Anglia, the Tarzans of dear old Langley Wood.

After a good drive and the consequent fusillade of shots, we gathered up the bagged birds, hares and rabbits, and assembled at the point where the game wagon would arrive to collect the guns. If the wagon was not at some remote glade, we carried the game ourselves, in braces according to species; pheasants, partridges, woodcock, and sometimes wood pigeons. We would slit the hocks of hares and rabbits on one hind leg and, after pushing the other hind through the slit, hook them over our beating sticks and shoulder carry them to Walton's Park. Shoots were always planned so that we would be near there at one o'clock. We were supplied with bread and cheese and a couple of bottles of beer apiece, while the guns, as guests of the squire, enjoyed luncheon, beautifully cooked by Miss Hawes. Chris and the lads would try to outdo each other's cunning in the collection of spent cartridge cases, ranging from 12 bore to 20 bore, of many different bright colours according to manufacture. These were their trophies of the chase and, fastened into belts of bellbine, they wore them like Mexican brigands.

Langley Wood and the outlying coverts would be beaten and shot in the forenoon, leaving Home Wood, the parkland copses and fields for the shorter spell in the afternoon. Punctually at two o'clock Rodwell would rouse us. 'Come you on, tergither. Best be a-movin'. Bob! Bugger an' blast yer bloody owd hide!' This to his dog, making slyly for the kitchen door to pick up scraps put out for him by Connie and Winnie, the housemaids.

Thus we would move off for the final drives of the day in advance of the guns. At a whistle, which assured Rodwell that guns were ready and waiting, the old keeper would yell his command.

'Git a-gooin', then. Make plenty o' row.'

Hitching his big shooting bag to a more comfortable position, he would dive into the undergrowth, the happiest of men; for this was the gamekeeper's harvest home; the anthem was the rattle of sticks, shouts from beaters, whirring wings, sharp shots in frosty air, delighted yelps from setters, pointers and retrievers, before the giving of alms.

After the final crashes from guns we all assembled in the kitchen yard to lay out the bag on stable cobblestones. There were arguments about the best shot; who had gained most, with the least barrels. Then some of us would stow away the bag in the game larder.

Major Luddington never failed to thank us, or to commiserate if the going had been hard, as he handed Rodwell our reward. Eight shillings each for a day off from farm labouring (at 12s a week) – man and boy alike, and a brace of rabbits, and for the ammunition carriers an extra half-crown. We were not allowed to touch firearms, but in view of the prospective tip there was much rivalry over who should carry the cartridge bags.

9
Country crafts

Young Benjam Batchin, wen he wor a lad,
He used tew goo thatchin' alonger his dad,
What taught him tew do ut as clever as he.
(A masterly thatcher wor owd mister B.)

But th' boy fell tew smokin' an' thet duden't match
Alonger his business o' larnin' tew thatch.
Th' owd man he mobbed him; but it worn't no use,
Th' young 'un wor gettin' tew big fer his boots.

Although his dad towed him, again an' again,
He wor thatchin' one day an' he set ut a-flame.
He set on the ridgin' an' hollered like mad,
'Same's a scaryfoid pidgin,' remarked his owd dad.

'Thet shud teach him a lesson, an' give him more sense,'
The owd man went on, as he leant on the fence.
'Oi 'spose by th' roights Oi shud let him remain,
But the Lard God hedd marcy, an' brought down th' rain.'

Prentice hand WILLIAM F. DOOLEY (1906–)

William Smith, or Owd Cribby as we called him, was the roadman of our parish. He was dwarfish, elfish and bent like a human question mark from continual stooping at his work. His eyes were as blue as cornflowers and his cheeks shone like ripe cherries through wisps of his old man's beard. He was a kindly man and much admired in Bartlow Hamlet. He kept our village spick and span. Throughout the seasons he trundled his council barrow along the inferior roads, all a-bristle with trimming hooks, distorted sickles, scythe, besom broom, shovel, mattock and various hoes and edge trimmers. In summer there were slender hazel wands as well, with paper windmills pinned at their ends, for the children. One of his legs was two inches shorter than the other. He envied the children's running as he jerked and bobbed along in pain, but he loved them all.

Our road was made from flints grouted with loam and well rolled down. In winter it was a morass, deeply rutted and pot-holed. Alongside were heaps of flintstones from which Cribby took shovelfuls to repair the ravages. Carts and wagons passing from field to farm rutted the road. Their wheels brought mud. Cribby loved mud. 'It's good growin' soil, bor!' he would say. He scraped it from the roads, packed it down on hedge-banks and verges, and when it had dried and he had made it tilthy, he planted it with primroses, violets, buttercups, daisies and even dandelions. They made his work shine in the spring.

Cribby was always dressed the same; homely corduroys with knee straps (wallies), clod-hopping boots, a striped flannelette shirt with celluloid collar zebra-striped in verticals of black and white, attached to the neckband by a brass stud which painted his Adam's apple green. His hat was shapeless and had been a gift from a parson. He called it his 'halo'. Cribby had a large family, five sons and three daughters. Ephraim and Walter worked on the land with my grandfather Reuben Ford and Brassy Stalley at Overhall Farm. His daughter Nellie had raven black hair and was full of fun with bright lights in her dark eyes. When we pulled her plaits she never yelled like the other girls, she punched.

Throughout his long life Cribby worked upon, and was solely responsible for, eight miles of highway, and long stretches of lanes and by-ways. At harvest time he also helped one of the farmers. He kept chickens and pigs, his garden was a model of good husbandry, and he had saved to buy his house, which he kept in good repair. Sometimes in summer the Rural District Surveyor decided to reline a stretch of road. Although this meant that Cribby had to forego his 'harvest money', he would be jubilant, because he would be 'in charge'.

As boys we were always intrigued by the road mending. Strange vehicles came. The clanking water cart, the puffing steam roller. Cribby supervised the deep sprinkling of flints on the surface before great quantities of earth were spread over them. But the big thrill was to watch the steam roller, to listen to its pantings and groanings as the black-faced driver switched it to reverse. Then the water cart sprayed the earth in sunshine with hundreds of rainbowy streams before the roller came into action. We would try to count the rotations of the big governor balls and watch water squirt in muddy streams from the roller's edges as it moved slowly backwards and forwards until the earth and flints were pounded flat. Cribby was in his element as he brushed surplus water into gullies and ditches with his springy besom, bellowing out instructions like fury. 'Howd hard, there. Not tew fierce, now. Yew'll scratch the sufface!' Then, to the roller driver, 'Quick, now, quick. Afore the water seeps in!'

Later, granite replaced the flint, but years passed before we knew macadam. With the new materials Cribby's task was lightened, but he still had to deal with mud brought in from fields. His hours were six in the morning until six in the evening, unless it was too dark to see, summer and winter alike. He was twisted and tortured by rheumatism, the legacy of his calling, and used to remark, 'That owd cure fer the screws is all me eye an' Betty Martin.' The cure was supposed to be a mixture of mushroom leaves and roadman's sweat. 'There's plenty o' sweat, drat it, but ye see, bor, mushrooms ain't got nary a leaf!'

Most farmers kept large flocks of sheep for wool and mutton, and for fertilising the fields, and they had to be kept to their own areas by hurdle boundaries. There was a big demand for repairs or renewals of hurdles and the hurdlemaker was fully occupied throughout the year. The three Marsh brothers carried on a flourishing trade as hurdlemakers and were famous, until the outbreak of the 1914 war. Walter, the hero of the agricultural strike, a reservist, was the first to go, then James; but Nipper was a conscientious objector and remained to carry on the trade single handed. His yard was by the

Bricklayer's Arms and it was always filled with newly made hurdles and large stacks of ashpoles. Nipper was ever ready to admit how much he missed the exceptionally powerful arm of Walt for riving the poles. Walt always made the job look easy and earned the praise of his brothers. 'There ain't nobody as can rive a pole like Walt, I don't care who he is.'

In winter the hurdlemaker could be seen on his way to woods and hedgerows, where magnificent trees peculiar to England marked field boundaries in the distant landscape. He did not look for shredded pollard elms, great oaks, maples, cedars, beeches, birches, aspens, or the olive green willow; he was after ash trees and would find the best saplings in deep glades of the woods. Ash was used exclusively in making five-barred hurdles. After hewing the poles and transporting them to his cottage yard, he cut them into lengths for riving by skilful use of the 'throw', a heavy nine inch blade of great strength attached at an angle of ninety degrees to a short wooden handle, like a massive cut-throat razor. The blade was hammered into the end grain of the pole to be rived, then by sheer strength of the forearm the cleavage was continued until the pole was split into two equal parts. This was repeated until the pole was reduced to rails 2 in wide by 1 in thick.

The two upright frames were cut more thickly, for they were the ends and the main supports of the five rails. The bottom ends were sharpened with a billhook to points to drive into the soil, and the inner sides morticed; one end of the rails was driven into the mortices and secured with cut nails, and by this simple method any rail could be replaced without affecting the rest of the hurdle. A metal shackle was slipped over the frame and the other end of the rails made secure, then two diagonal braces were fixed for extra strength, from the centre downwards. The hurdle was then ready to hand over to the shepherd, who erected it in the field, driving a stake through the shackle. The shackle was slipped over the frame of the next hurdle to form another link in the hurdle chain. Hurdles were erected so that they slightly overlapped. When the stake was driven in, connecting hurdles would be fixed almost immovably in the ground. This was essential. Penned sheep are restive and rub their considerable weight against the hurdles.

The standard hurdle for East Anglia was 6 ft long by 3 ft or 4 ft high. The construction never varied but there were different requirements to suit a particular farmer, and to create gates and openings. Gates were made slightly heavier and required a different shackle fastened to a smaller loop, which passed over a hooked end and was secured like a safety pin. The shepherd unhooked the small loop and lifted the end of the hurdle to open the gate.

The stakes were provided by the hurdle maker from 5 ft to 6 ft lengths of ash, the bottom pointed and the top chamfered to fit the shallow metal head of the shepherd's mallet. This helped to drive the stake into the ground and also prevented the head from splintering and burring.

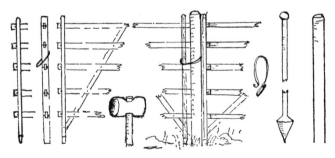

The hurdlemaker spent the winter months collecting and repairing damaged hurdles. Sometimes he took them to his yard, but more likely to an open farm shed, where slivers of newly shaved ash and stacks of repaired hurdles reared high and wide. He needed only the simplest cutting tools, a small billhook or two, a small axe, one or two larger ones, a mortice chisel, saw, draw knife; the single edged steel blade of the draw knife was a good foot long with a round knob at each end which he grasped in each hand, pulling the knife towards him to shave the wood; and of course the throw, and tucked away in his frail basket a hammer and a wooden mallet for the final fixing. All his tools had razor sharp edges and were kept honed on whetstones and oilstones.

His cradle was a tripod trestle terminating in a forked top, the whole leaning at an acute angle away from the working point. On this the ash pole was laid, the end protruding through the fork, and getting into a comfortable position for riving, he would split it into rails.

It was a sight to see the apparent ease with which Walter Marsh worked, the cleavage running exactly along the line dictated by pressure of arm on the handle of the throw; to watch the dexterous twist of his wrist and the rippling muscles was to appreciate the expert he was. He would split ash poles of great girth through the centre for stockyard fences, and long poles for side posts of ladders, as accurately as a saw, so that they only needed a little smoothing with the plane. 'Allus wuk with the grain...Never goo furrin to the grain,' he would say.

The demand for hurdles diminished as farmers sold their flocks. The war disrupted everything, and the farmer became his own shepherd when the men went off to war. After the war James and Walter returned to help Nipper revive the business, and to give them a chance Nipper took a job as a road ganger away from the village. But still the trade declined, and James and Walter went to work on the land. Walter was nearly ninety when I last saw him on a fleeting visit. Sitting on the wall near the Rose and Crown at the centre of the village, his short blackened clay pipe dripped with a moist dottle and was all but empty, but Ron Huckle and I bought tobacco from the old grocery for him and his friend. His eyes were bright as new horse chestnuts. 'Good ter see ye, Ced, bor. Glad ter see yer. Things ain't what they wor. Got metal hardles now, on wheels. I reckon if I see another ten year they'll be hevin' metal sheep an' all!'

We had our own skilled and hard working hay and straw tyers. This family craft was allied to the seasonal work of rick and stack thatching, and their services were in full demand at hay time and harvest. Our farmers grew surplus quantities of hay and straw which found ready markets with neighbouring livery stables, and huge loads were sent in haywains and wagons to stables and mews in London.

Fingers were used to comb the straw to make sure the bundles were uniform and did not stray out at the ends. It was then tied with straw ropes, two to a bale, and combed and raked again before being stacked to await transportation. Careful loading was essential as many towns the haywains passed through had by-laws against littering the highway.

Trussing hay involved the use of a heavy press. Built on a sturdy oak frame, it comprised a rectangular platform with a lid loosely held by balance weights, and was mounted on two road wheels and drawn by horse from farm to farm. The tyer cut into a haystack with his sharp hay-knife to extract neat squares or rectangles of hay to fit the press (experienced cutters did this accurately by judgment). He threw the whole of his weight on a long thick shaft of oak in a kind of pumping action which operated a ratchet, and this forced down the lid to compress the hay into trusses. The work was extremely arduous. Hay tyers were strong men, they had to be, even though some of them were not heavy. When the truss was fully pressed, strong twine was threaded round it with a special needle and securely knotted, then it was lifted clear to be trimmed with thatching shears.

From sunrise to sunset, and sometimes until dark, the operation was repeated. Tyers knew exactly how many trusses made a ton weight. Expert judges of quality, they knew the difference in weight between good and bad hay, and never pressed inferior hay. They might have been tempted to do so, for they were paid by tonnage, but the need to preserve their integrity was paramount, and when the day was done considerable amounts of discarded hay were left lying about. They knew the privations and grinding poverty that went hand in hand with unemployment, and worked until there was no work left in them.

We were a bit scared of Mossy Harris, the first of our hay and straw tyers. Gaunt and rangy, perched high on the saddle of a penny-farthing bicycle, his unkempt hair streaming in the wind, he careered at a great lick along our flinty roads. Sparks shot out every few yards from the worn out tyres. A murderous looking hay-knife strapped across his shoulders did nothing to detract from his fearsome appearance. Those who knew him best said old Mossy could only ride his bone-shaker when he was drunk, for it was only then that he had the courage to mount into the high saddle. He followed his trade sporadically, and owing to his prowess as a poacher it was often interrupted by spells in Cambridge gaol. He did not live long, but remains a colourful memory.

Herb (Cockerel) Fisher was another straw tyer. His work took him deep into Cambridgeshire, and he pedalled furiously with hay-knife and two-tined fork lashed to the cross bar of his bicycle. Spare, tough, sinewy and extremely active, he worked alone unless lent a farmhand where he was employed.

The most colourful thatcher and tyer we knew was 'Brother' Joslin, a notorious hot-gospeller, slight, wiry, but with amazing strength. He was dedicated to his job. Invariably, he wore knee pads fashioned from sacking, pin-striped trousers secured with bicycle clips, and over these he sometimes wore a pair of his wife's bloomers, purple socks, occasionally a beret, or a mothy top hat. His unorthodox dress and pronounced stutter made him an object of ridicule, but he always wore a cheerful smile and an air of Baptist sanctity.

Farmhands and children baited him unmercifully, but Brother was tolerant and forgiving, and if a man cursed or blasphemed, he would get down on his sack-padded knees and pray. It was said that his knees were padded more for prayer than for protection against the normal hazards of thatching, but Brother did a lot of both. He toiled ceaselessly to the rhythm of the hymns and psalms he bellowed out full throttle. After he had finished thatching he always stood on his head and hands on the ridge of a rick to sing a song of upside-down praises.

Like Cockerel, Brother worked alone. He would borrow a helper only when he spun straw ropes to bind his bundles. For this he used a swingle, a tool similar to a carpenter's brace, with a cranked handle, but with a metal hook instead of a chuck. He put a handful of straw on the hook, and while the helper turned the swingle he twisted the straw skilfully into a long tenuous rope. Sometimes he sang his 'rope song' . . . 'Throw out the lifeline, someone is sinking today.' Then he carefully looped each rope over a pattern of hazel stakes driven into the earth, to prevent curling and tangling.

The tyers are all gone now. One press they used to work leans bent and distorted in a nettle-infested corner of a battery-breeding farmyard, its timbers warped and rotted. Iron wheels are rusted immovably to the axle, encrusted with moss and fungus, the ratchet handle awry across the lid. A mute memorial.

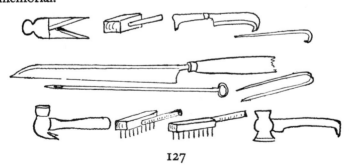

The ancient trade of thatching in use in Norfolk, Suffolk and Essex is of two kinds, reed and straw, but there are many variations of style and trim. Norfolk reed, which lasts much longer, has a finer finish and lends itself to artistic decoration. Straw is more pliable and readily adapted to hipped roofs, curving dormers and other undulations. Wheat and rye are the best straws for house thatching, but of course both are vulnerable to fire and ravaging by birds. As a counter to fire old thatchers used to treat straw with a solution of water and alum. To frustrate birds they laid a fine-meshed wire netting over the finished thatch, but this was expensive.

Reed thatching belongs almost exclusively to Suffolk and Norfolk, where reed and peat were for long the two characteristic products. Local thatchers considered Norfolk reed superior both in length and pliancy to that of Dorsetshire and Kent. For reed thatching the pitch of the roof must be high to keep a good rain slope, and weight must be sufficient to bat it down close with the heavy slope-ended mallet. Heavy stakes are laid between the groynes, and reeds are laid on from the eaves upwards in wide strips, as far as arms can reach. Osier pegging was once preferred to hazel springles[1] because willow grows profusely in Norfolk, but later there has been a preference for stitching, using long steel tie needles and tarred twine.

Most Essex cottages thatched in reed owe their thatches to the Norfolk craftsmen, who brought their own reeds and tools and a dialect which was a source of merriment to Essex children. We would hear our own straw thatcher long before we saw him, high on the roof of rick, barn or cottage, as he hammered home the hazel sprindles[2] to secure the straw to the ridge. Blows from his mallet sounded muffled but purposeful from the top of his forty-rung ladder. Now and again he came to do a bit of patching, sometimes to strip an old thatch to

[1] springles, split hazel rods
[2] Sprindles, also split hazel rods, are split thinly and cut to 2 ft lengths, the ends sharpened with longer points.

replace laths and straw throughout, a task which exercised the skills of other craftsmen too, the hurdlemaker to split laths from long ash poles, the blacksmith to hammer out steel needles and fastening hooks.

We would check his progress on our way to school as he placed a new coating of thatch on Aunt Jane's, or the Keeper's Cottage, or on a completely new roof. Laths were nailed at 1 ft centres in continuous lines along the length of the roof, to form a platform for thick layers of straw. While the thatcher busily secured his battens, his mate below prepared the great heaps of straw glistering in the morning sunlight; these he continually soaked with rain water, shook up, and turned and turned again with a two-tined pitchfork to ensure equal drenching.

Yelving was a back breaker. I found this out when I helped my father to thatch the cornricks at Ashdon Place Farm. It was a hand and back job at the stoop, the fingers of both hands fully distended and kept rigid, the palms turned in towards the yelver, who then rapidly stroked a bundle of well wetted straw drawn up close to his feet, using his fingers like the teeth of a comb, alternating to right and left. By this process the thatcher ensured that eventual layers of straw carried rain outwards and downwards and would not soak through the depth of the thatch. After yelving, the helper took up his bridle, a hand made contraption of two yard lengths of wood one inch thick, loosely coupled with stout cord. He placed layers of straw diagonally on the bottom wand, until there was sufficient to keep the thatcher busy while more straw was being yelved. The second wand was then brought over and secured tightly with the cord to the bottom wand.

The big bundle was easily carried up the ladder, and the diagonal staggering enabled the thatcher to pick up one layer at a time without disturbing the remainder. Along the length of the eaves the prepared straw was laid to the appropriate thickness, and a long pliant hazel rod laid over the thatch and pinned down with iron hooks made by the blacksmith, which were hammered into the rafters. Working from left to right, or right to left, according to his hand, he laid the rest of the thatch. After the first layers, instead of pinning with iron hooks he used a long tie needle threaded with strong tarred twine, thrusting it through the thatch to a mate working below who passed it round a rafter or batten and thrust it back. This was continued for the length of the hazel rod, and by a system of knotting and tying the thatch was held securely in place. Layering and stitching was repeated until the thatch reached the ridge.

Great care was taken over capping the ridge. Long lengths of split hazel rods (springles) were placed at close intervals and driven home with the mallet. With a dexterous twist at the centre the thatcher bent them into staples which were driven into the close packed thatch.

Having secured the ridge the thatcher cut out in relief a series of ornamental points in the patterns and designs which were his trade mark. Using a long-handled tool with scythe-like blade (most ill-balanced and unwieldy for the layman) he trimmed up, making the cleanest of cuts and the straightest of edges to finish off. He descended his ladder, lit up his old clay pipe, and took a long look. If satisfied, he raked down the whole area to remove loose straws, and the job was done. The thatch would last a good fifty years.

A 'buildings' thatcher was not often called to thatch corn ricks, but left this simpler task to farm thatchers, who were equally efficient if less artistic. The problems of rick thatches were of comparatively short term, they had to keep rain and birds from corn until threshing time, two years at most. Sometimes a rick was covered with wire mesh to keep out the corn bunting, which penetrated thatch when winter was severe, and food other than stacked wheat hard to come by. They made small holes in the thatch, wriggled through them, pulled out wheat ears, and ate the grain on the stack. This was not much to worry about, but they left the tell-tale signs, the husks, as invitations to bigger and hungrier birds.

All the farms were rat-infested. The rapacity of rats was costly, for in addition to the cereals they consumed they also destroyed vast quantities of corn. Stockyards reeked of rats and mice. Chicken huts constructed with slatted floors were ideal nesting places. In the erroneous belief that pigs would become immune from rheumatism if bedded on wood, farmers had the floors of sties made of thick planks or sleepers. These were even better breeding places for the rats. After the pigs had eaten and gone to sleep they would come out to feed from the troughs. It was common to see gigantic, mangy old bucks, their filthy hides scarred from combat, and tiny pink nestlings only a few days old scrambling over the troughs, ready to flash or scramble back to their lairs at the slightest alarm. In meal sheds where stockmen mixed cattle bait there were rat droppings, rat runs, and always their characteristic stench. In storage barns where sacks of grain were stacked there were no outward signs of molestation, but when the sacks were moved corn gushed from large holes in the bottom. Sometimes the whole store had to be sacked and weighed afresh, and spare sacks stored beyond rat reach. Bundles of them would be slung over ropes suspended from cross-beams, as were tarpaulins and rain covers for agricultural machinery. Rats would gnaw anything, of food value or not – ladder rungs, wooden steps and wooden handles of tools – and some farms were so heavily infested that one could scarcely look in any direction without seeing a rat. Many methods were employed to keep them down – ferreting, shooting, snaring, poisoning and trapping – with partial success. But in Ashdon and adjacent parishes farmers would eventually send to Great Chesterford for Billy Mason, whose smell lingered in many nostrils. Sometimes called the Pied Piper of Chesterford, his importance was not lost on him. Time and again he would remind us, 'Where there be farm buildin's there be pigs an' chickens. Where there be pigs an' chickens there'll allus be rats an' meece. S'long as they get 'em I 'on't never be outer wuk. Oi'm the bloody rat-kitcher!' It was reassuring to see Billy making his way around infested buildings, long-handled spoon held in readiness like a rifle, canvas bag filled with meal or grain. Time and again he would dip his spoon into the bag, carefully measuring the amount of bait he inserted into holes and runs, beyond the reach of domestic animals. For three consecutive days Billy would lay his bait, never missing a hole that was in use by the rat colony. He fed his prey on a dish of his own concoction which they relished. On the fourth day, having taken careful stock of the disappearance of previous deposits, he would bait the holes with meal dosed with a virulent poison. Next day he would go on his round again, to pick up dead rats by the score. Many more would be dead in their burrows.

Farmhands said that as Billy moved round the corn ricks on his final tour, rats and mice fell dead in his wake. It was also said that if Billy did not receive a liberal reward for his specialist services, he could arrange for the rats to multiply instead of diminishing. The Pied Piper of Chesterford could 'make the buggers come an' goo as he thowt fit'. Billy was always well paid in beer, food and hard cash. He mixed his 'speshul pisens' from herbs he gathered in the woods, and never divulged his secrets.

10

Old wives' tales

A good huswife provides, ere sickness do come,
Of sundry good things in her house to have some;
Good aqua composita, vinegar tart,
Rose water and treacles, to comfort thine heart.
Cold herbs in her garden for agues that burn,
That over-strong heat to good temper may turn.
White endive and succory, spinnach enow;
All such, with good pot herbs, should follow the plough.
Conserves of barbary, quinces and such,
With sirops that easeth the sickly so much.
Good broth, and good keeping do much now and than,
Good diet, with wisdom, best comforteth man.
In health, to be stirring shall profit thee best;
In sickness, hate trouble; seek quiet and rest.
   Remember thy soul, let no fancy prevail;
   Make ready for God-ward; let faith never quail.
   The sooner thyself thou submittest to God,
   The sooner He ceaseth to scourge with his rod.

Housewifely physic THOMAS TUSSER (1523–80)

Bewhiskered, weather-stained and nearing sixty, grandfather Reuben Ford tethered his plough team to a five-barred gate to eat his dockey (elevenses). His sharp shutknife conveyed to his mouth a sliver of cheese topped with raw onion, and he pointed to the lower half of a cottage loaf made the day before by Granny Ford in the 'bakus' behind our twin cottages, Brick and Stone Villa. 'With half a quartern o' that, a mite o' cheese and an' owd onion I can larst the day,' and he washed down a mouthful with a gulp of home-brewed ale.

Bread was our staple diet. Every cottage housewife was taught by her mother the art of mixing, firing, kneading and watching, to make loaves and bakestones in brick ovens. There was an immediate restoration of energy from a hunk or two, with or without butter, cheese or the hard butcher's dripping.

For the fortnightly ritual of baking Granny Susannah Ford prepared her dough overnight, placing careful measures of white wheat flour in her kneading trough, the keeler. Secret measures of salt and water were added and a little mysterious 'something' to the yeast, a family secret. When thoroughly mixed the wooden lid of the keeler was pressed down and covered with warmed sacks to assist fermentation. By morning the rising dough would have forced off the lid. Pressing firmly but gently all over the sacking with the flat of her hands to expel the gases, Susannah would then get busy shaping and moulding on the upturned well-floured lid; a tidy lump for the base, a small one for the top, and the shape of the cottage loaf was formed.

Meanwhile Reuben, after feeding Overhall Farm's horses, brought the oven to baking heat. The correct temperature was of paramount importance. Deep inside the clay-plastered oven was placed an ignited faggot of dead and well-dried black-thorn or whitethorn. Carefully directed jets of air from hand bellows drew the fire to an even white heat on which branches of whitethorn were continually thrust until they became white hot. The right time for putting the dough in the oven was determined by a glance at the 'watch and tell-tale', a small pebble specially selected from the fields, which changed colour with variations of temperature. This was built into the oven. When it became fiery red embers were raked into the recess below the oven which was then cleaned with a mop made of sacking tied to a pole and saturated with water. One at a time each loaf was placed in the oven with a peel, a long spoon of circular board mounted on a wooden handle, and left to bake. Granny then scrubbed down the keeler (a much-prized gift from the wheelwright on her wedding day) and would stand sniffing the wonderful smell of baking bread; by this she knew when it was properly baked. Then sliding a steel-bladed peel under the loaves, she removed them one at a time to the deal table to cool. Her fortnightly baking was over, and we would get hot bread to sample, smelling of wheat and heat softened cheese.

But there were other rituals to be observed. Not a bit of the oven's heat could be wasted for faggots were cut by hand and carried from woods and hedgerows, or were sixpence a piece to buy. Therefore King Edward potatoes were placed in the heart of the glowing embers. Never since have baked potatoes tasted so good. Pots and pans and pails filled with water followed them into the still hot copper over the oven, for baking day was also bath day. The whole family, often two at a time, stood in turn in a zinc bath, washing away a fortnight's dirt.

But twice a year the bakehouse copper was used for an event of great consequence, ale day. Licking his lips, surrounded by odd-sized sacks of berries, hops, malt and yeast, Reuben wished not to be disturbed by man or beast as he brought twenty-four gallons of spring water to the boil. He poured it over the malt in the keeler, gave furious stirrings, then added sugar and hops. When cool it was sampled by adults and children alike, at the stage of the 'sweet wat', but we were not encouraged to drink much of it for it was intended for the workmen in the fields and, if good enough, for entry in the fête or flower show. This sweet wat was brought back to the boil before yeast was added and left to settle for four or five hours, after which the strong brown ale was strained into casks, enough to last through seed time to harvest. Other than the zinc and copper containers, everything used in ale brewing was homemade; keelers, stirring paddles, ladles, casks and taps.

Few utensils were required for Granny Ford's wine making: tubs obtained from the publican for a shilling and sawn in half to make two mashers; a few stone jars ranging from half a gallon to four gallons, and some wooden casks.

After careful sorting and cleaning, the roots, flowers or fruit were immersed in cold spring water and left for several weeks. From time to time the scum forming on the surface was skimmed. When ready, the juice was strained through fine muslin into the jars; demerara sugar was added, and the juice was put in an iron boiler and heated. The sweetened liquid was poured into a cask, stirred and left to ferment. Some people used brewer's yeast to aid fermentation, either by dissolving it in the liquid, or by placing yeast on a slice of toast and letting it float on the surface for several days. After standing for a prescribed period, according to the variety of fruit, the wine was poured into broaching casks, and corked loosely to allow it to breathe. After fermentation corks and bungs were driven home, and final instructions were given ... 'That marn't be meddled oo fer a year or more. Wine ain't wine till it's seen a couple o' buthdays!'

Although elderberries were profuse and easily gathered they were not much used for wine making in the 1920s. Our bread was spread with elderberry jam during the Kaiser's War, and we were sick of it. But our folk in Bartlow Hamlet were expert in making six favourites from field, allotment and meadow; parsnip, rhubarb, wheat, dandelion, barley and cowslip. There were many others, including bee, potato and carrot. My favourite was Granny Ford's hip wine, like a fine liqueur. Joslin the thatcher did not think much of the last three ... 'Don't seem to tickle the owd gizzard much, my brethren!' Granny had a little book which she passed on to my mother, all creased and fruit stained.

COWSLIP

Gather 2 pecks of cowslips.
Lay to dry in sun for a few days.
Take 18 quarts spring water.
To each gallon of water add 3 lb raw sugar – put on fire.
When nearly boiling put in well-beaten whites of 2 eggs.
Boil 1 hour.
Allow to cool.
When lukewarm put in cowslips, juice, and peel of 3 lemons and 2 tablespoons yeast.

Stir well twice daily for 3 or 4 days.
When fermentation ceases strain through sieve into barrel.
Bung closely.
Stand for nearly 1 month.
NB: If bottling add 1 lump sugar to each bottle.

DANDELION

4 lb dandelion heads	1 orange
(gathered in sun)	3 lb loaf sugar
3 quarts cold water	1 lemon

Boil flower heads with thinly peeled fruit rinds for 30 minutes.
Place sugar, sliced lemon and sliced orange into large bowl.
Strain off juice into bowl and stir well.
When lukewarm, stir in yeast.
Leave for 3 days.
Strain into jars, cork lightly until fermentation ceases.
Secure cork.
NB: The longer kept the better. Good tonic and pick-me-up.

These were the wines offered to friends and relations to wash down a hunk of seed cake. There were nods and comments of approval if it was good. 'That's more-ish,' and the empty glass would be pushed forward for refilling. Silence was a condemnation.

But there was a wine made by an old man at Camps End, who claimed it had the power of palliatives, the punch of purgatives and the balm of balsam; it would cure whooping cough, ingrowing toe-nails, bring out the rashes of measles and chickenpox, but above all it was the world's best aphrodisiac ... 'It's powerful, bor. Makes weak men strong, an' strong men impossible. Yew ask the gels!'

The wine was made from the roots of comfrey, a tall ditch plant with very rough leaves and clusters of bell-like white and purple flowers.

COMFREY

Dig roots, wash thoroughly, peel and slice into strips.
Put in pan and add water, 1 gallon to each 4 roots.
Boil with lid off until roots are soft (roots stink).
Strain liquid through muslin and throw away roots.
Add to liquid 3 lb preserving sugar.
Simmer 1 hour.
Pour liquid into earthenware jar.
Allow to cool (lukewarm).
Add brewer's yeast on toast, about 1 oz.
Cover with cloth and stir daily for 10 days.
When finished working (fermenting) pour into cask or jar.
Leave for 3 months.
Throw away pulp, add sugar and lemon juice, leave to
ferment for a little over a week.
Strain and bottle, leaving cork free.
As it ferments keep bottle filled until fermentation ceases
(surplus liquid should be kept for this purpose).
When wine is at rest, with no more fermentation, tighten
cork.

'Doan't yew dare bring that in, 'cos I 'on't hev it. Tha's
unlucky tew hev in housen, laylock allus wor!' Chris's Aunt
Sukey gave vehement emphasis to the belief she shared with
most village folk, that white lilac was unlucky if taken into the
house. Elder blossom, may blossom – both red and white –
bluebells, honeysuckle, ivy, maidenhair grass and the
hydrangea were all harbingers of bad tidings. Treacherous was
the elm, for without visible rot or disease, its limbs could fall
on folk taking shelter under its branches. The twisted and
distorted grain (warped by the Devil) of the wych elm was a
magnet for witches, cypresses meeting places for evil spirits –
usually in graveyards. The elder was lucky as well as unlucky,
the one and only tree to afford protection against lightning,
evil spirits, drought and poor crops; but ill fortune would

follow if it was cut, sawn or burnt after dark. If hung in the hall, holly would ward off witches, but it should never be cut or burnt, because, believed to be the tree on which Christ was crucified, Christ's blood and tears would flow with the sap. Willow should never be brought indoors if cut with saws. Billhooks, sickles and other edged tools cut the willow without making it weep. Saw-cuts brought sap and tears, and sorrow.

Among the few symbols of good luck two held prominence: the black cat and the chimney sweep. Brides were encouraged to stroke the former and kiss the latter. If hung in the room where the family ate meals, a spray of hops in flower would ensure the household's prosperity. If found in fields (not on roads) after horses had cast them, horseshoes were lucky – provided they were cast over the left shoulder and no attempt was made to find where they had fallen. Fixed over the cottage door, they invited good luck, and the good Lord, to enter; it was essential to nail up the shoe with its horns pointing heavenwards, otherwise luck would 'run down' and the Devil would intrude.

Every village child knew one old rhyme, believed every word of it, and would search great areas of meadowland in the hope of discovery . . .

> If you find a four-leaved clover,
> All your trouble will be over.

The monkey-puzzle tree with its dark green spiked leaves – one of which grew in the parson's garden – was believed to be more puzzling to the Devil than to monkeys. Sunday-school children who lagged in learning, or played hookey, had but to climb this tree and the Devil, if not parsons and parents, would never catch them. Dark yew trees were frighteners, particularly at night, when ghosts, witches and earth-bound spirits lurked in their gloom, ready to pounce upon the un-baptised and those who dodged Holy Communion.

The moon figured extensively in the village's beliefs. To

ensure good luck throughout its phases, females were expected to bow or curtsey 'towards the sickle' when the first sliver of the new moon appeared. If first seen through glass, misfortune would attend throughout the phases of the next two moons, irrespective of the number of curtsies made in its direction. A coin in the pocket of a person first sighting the crescent of a new moon should be turned over for luck. There were various omens and portents about the position of the new moon. If 'sleeping', on its back, or ringed, bad weather would follow. If 'up on its tail', particularly at harvest time, every farmer was pleased, for good weather would last. To sleep with undrawn curtains with the moon shining on one's face, was an invitation to nightmares and ultimate lunacy. Gardeners were convinced that seeds sown at new moon germinated more quickly than at other times; and whatever weather prevailed at the waxing would persist until the waning. Butchers and pig owners also kept a wary eye open; no one would dream of slaughtering a pig after the moon had 'passed its full'. All held rigidly to sayings and beliefs which had been handed down over the generations.

> A Saddidy moon an' Sunday full,
> Never wor no good, an' never wull.

A countrywoman setting off to market would fear to meet a cross-eyed person. Bad luck would follow, unless she returned home and started off again. It was also believed that if she met a woman first it would be disastrous for her business, if a man, everything would be well and her transactions would be profitable. To see a solitary magpie also heralded misfortune, but if more birds appeared at once the bad luck would be reversed. Although owls abounded and were common sights, if one heard the long drawn-out hoot of a tawny owl, and it was not at once repeated, one could be sure that a near friend or relative had died at that moment. Consequently, the exact time of the hoot was carefully noted. Coincidental bereavements strengthened this belief. Toads were regarded with misgiving, and none would disturb them. Known to be beneficial to gardens, they were reputed to possess the 'evil eye' and should not be provoked. Some species of caterpillar were held in dread. If touched, and no one ever touched to find out, the furry one known as the 'Davel's Ring' was reputed to coil itself round the toucher's finger, and could only be removed by witchcraft.

No village housewife would change sheets, turn mattresses, or trim her nails, or allow any member of the family to do so, on Fridays and Sundays. Friday was 'Black Day', the day the sun was blotted out, the curtain rent in twain, and Christ had died. Sunday being holy, if not so sad, it would raise the Devil himself if nails were pared and beds turned on that day.

Every village in the locality was said to harbour a witch. Night-flying bats were their agents and spell carriers, and wreaked the witch's will upon subjects of her animosity. Consequently, cottage windows were firmly closed at night and young ladies out a-wooing wore headscarves, 'fer fear o' gettin' bat mad'. 'On'y way ter git a bat owter the hair is ter cut it all orf, but part o' the brains comes with it.'

High swifts that shrieked shrilly in their divings and dartings round the church tower were viewed by older people with foreboding, 'Jacky Davels', they called them. Their twistings and sombre colour lent credence to their affinity with the Devil and the powers of darkness. But if a house-martin built its nest of mud under the eaves or gable-end of a cottage, the householder was cheered. Martins only built their nests where prosperity was about to enter and remain.

Elegant, delicate dragonflies were feared by women and children. Girls were told to avoid them. If they became tangled in the hair, the power and speedy threshing of their double wings – plus their hypnotic powers – would lure their victims to the nearest horse pond and drown them.

Superstition abounded about bees. Some were lucky, others not. The Dummy Dors, bigger and noisier than a bumble bee, was especially dreaded. If one flew into the house it had to be avoided to ensure no harm was intended towards it. The Dummy was supposed to foretell the visit of a stranger. The length of time it stayed in the room would correspond to the duration of the stranger's stay. When the owner of an apiary died, it was the bounden duty of some member of the household to don a black garment to inform the bees of the death. This was carried out by gently tapping each hive in turn, and quietly whispering, 'The master has passed on'. This was to assure the prosperity of the new owner. The bees would multiply and thrive. Failure to convey the message would result in the early death of all bees in the colony. The old adage, 'A swarm in May is worth a load of hay', was firmly believed. If a swarm was seen overhead in May, cottagers would dash to their gardens with tin trays, saucepan lids and table spoons, to bring down the swarm. Bees were regarded as belonging to the family. Flowers from brides' bouquets would be placed on hives after weddings, and sometimes wreaths after funerals. Some would go to the extent of draping the hives with black muslin, so that the bees could mourn with the family.

The robin was protected by superstition. Few would harm one. It was well known that to kill a robin invited a broken leg. If a robin flew indoors, or perched on a window sill, the winter would be hard. if hips and haws were profuse, too, winter would be hard. Seven years of bad luck would follow the breaking of a mirror. Bad luck for spilling salt could only be averted by throwing the salt over the left shoulder. Ill fortune attended crossed knives, scythes, saws and sickles, and walking under ladders. Children who picked dandelions would wet the bed. A stumble upstairs meant a wedding; to wear brown at social functions was unwise; funerals would follow. New clothes should be first worn on a Sunday, preferably to church, otherwise sackcloth and sorrow would follow. Brides should not marry in green. No one should sit under oak trees during thunderstorms. Never count between lightning's flash and thunder's clap to find out if the storm is coming or going.

Coloured flames in the fire foretold family illness. Sparks flying to hearth-rugs heralded the arrival of a letter from a distant reletive. You should never burn egg-shells, because thereafter the hen would lay only 'lush eggs' – without shells. A persistently crowing hen was as unpopular as a whistling woman. Falling pictures prophesied death. Christmas decorations should not be taken down before Epiphany. Opening an umbrella inside the house was bad luck. To put on a garment inside-out was fortunate, but only if accidental and the wearer wore it all day. Gifts of money or tips should be spat on for luck. Presents of pins, needles, brooches or knives could cut the friendship. This could be remedied by paying for them, a farthing would do. Dropped pins should be picked up. Weathercocks should be watched at noon on St Thomas's day. Wherever the wind happened to be at that time, it would remain for the following quarter.

Natural phenomena were always regarded with awe and apprehension. The Northern Lights were seen with great foreboding – some thought a national disaster was imminent, others that the end of the world was nigh. Comets were dreaded. Shooting stars foretold family deaths. Eclipse of sun or moon foretold different disasters; but all believed rainbows, mock suns, and suns with misty haloes heralded bad weather. According to report, most of our villagers thought the world was coming to an end on 27 May 1913, the hottest day of an early summer. All morning the sun had beaten down, then in the early afternoon a murky haze filled the sky, making the sun coppery instead of gold . . . 'It's the blight!' they surmised. There was an eerie stillness, birds stopped singing and hid in the trees, and nature seemed poised for some great calamity as the clouds thickened and shut out the light. Chris sat in school watching Mr Tuck and the other teachers, who were showing signs of unease. No one could settle down to work, and children's faces were pallid in the gathering gloom. Just after three o'clock an uncanny screaming noise was heard, and all the children clung to one another and the younger ones began to cry. Then came a devastating bombardment, which for years afterwards we knew as the 'Great Battering'. A nerve-shattering crash seemed to split the school roof, chunks of jagged ice crashed against the windows, and glass and broken tiles flew round the room. The school bell in the clock turret jangled as lumps of ice rebounding from the framework struck the casing. Hailstones the size of cricket balls were hitting the ground and rebounding to hit the low windows, and children's screams added to the din. Mercifully, there were no casualties.

When it began to get light again Mr Tuck sent his flock home. A scene of desolation met their eyes. The earth was covered with a carpet of melting ice. Overhanging the play-ground fence the once magnificent laburnum festooned with golden blossoms was reduced to scarred and splintered branches and bark slashed with long white streaks. Everywhere cottagers were inspecting and bemoaning the havoc wreaked on homes and gardens. Almost every window had been shattered, thousands of slates and tiles were broken, and even thatched roofs were badly damaged. All the trees were denuded of foliage. Fruit which had formed early in the genial weather lay ruined. The green corn was bowed and bent. Flowers had been shredded from beanstalks, making their pleasant smell seem even more delightful, but there would be no beans. Old Mr King, one time licensee of the Rose and Crown, had been out for his customary walk. Crippled with arthritis, he could only proceed at a snail's pace with two stout sticks. Because it was so hot he had gone out in shirtsleeves and an old straw hat. 'Kingy' was less than twenty yards from shelter when the storm struck. His straw hat was cut to pieces, his shirt shredded, his head badly gashed and his arms lacerated. He was shaken ... 'Ar. Oi thowt the Devil had got me at larst!' One farmer's horse team had bolted round the field and smashed up the plough, and Tom Webb, the ploughman, escaped with severe bruises. Old Riley the shepherd had a similar experience, for his cob bolted and overturned the cart, but he extricated the horse from its harness before taking shelter. At Walton's

Park not one pane of glass was left in the long range of green-houses built lean-to fashion against a brick wall. Long afterwards the mutilated bodies of wild birds were found around the fields. Chickens and game birds fared the same fate, for the fields and hedges offered little protection.

Ashdon bore the brunt of the storm. At Saffron Walden, five miles away, the hailstones were only the size of peas. At Castle Camps, a couple of miles in the opposite direction, they were the size of pigeon's eggs.

But there is one strange tale not much talked about, which belongs to our village. The stagnant pond behind the Manse is overhung with weeping willows and tall elms. It is a sombre place, so forbidding that few old folk will venture there, and won't go near it after dark. The legend goes that many years ago a 'lady of quality' was driving in her carriage and pair along the carriageway when forked lightning frightened the horses. They bolted, the carriage overturned, and the lady was thrown into the pond and drowned. Only a footpath remains of the carriageway – but the ghosts of the frightened horses and the drowned lady still haunt it. Lady Well is the only Ashdon pond where moorhens are never seen.

Whatever its superstitions may have been, Ashdon, like most villages, had one female upon whom every family relied. Mrs Fisher, who was given two apt names, 'mole catcher' and 'body snatcher', was a very small woman. A widow for many years, she lived alone in a cottage on the brow of Knox Hill. The majority of Ashdon's babies were delivered by her, usually without a doctor in attendance. 'Me time's a-comin', but I shall be all right. I've seen Mrs Fisher an' got bespoke.' Not only would she deliver the child, but for days after the birth she would attend to the other children of the family, run errands and do the cooking and washing until the vitality of the mother was restored. She also performed 'the last offices', as she called them, for the dead.

Miss Cant the district nurse lodged at Chris's step-uncle

Teddy Taylor's house, Clematis Cottage. When she arrived in 1918 she had few possessions other than her heavy bicycle and 'that owd bag o' trickery'. It would be difficult to find words to express the appreciation this young girl deserved. 'Our nurse', as we called her, had to serve other parishes and at all times of the day or night she was willing to answer any call, trivial or not. She would cycle many miles in all weathers along the flinty roads and tracks. After being up all night attending a maternity case, she would often return home just in time to receive another call, and cycle off again. We all loved her, and she found her niche and was happy. It was a pleasure to see her in her blue uniform as she spoke to a couple of old labourers in the fields. Her face would light up as she wished them good morning. They would straighten their bent backs, touch the peaks of their old caps, and say, 'Mornin', nuss, dear. A good day to ye,' and one would say to the other, 'Ain't she a little beauty? She's one o' WE.'

The nearest doctor lived at Saffron Walden, and drove the five miles in a pony trap. He came in emergencies by urgent request, often put off till the last moment because the household could not muster the half-crown bill. Visits and prescriptions had to be paid for, of course, and a bit extra for a night call.

In due course, Dr William Palmer, practising in Linton, Cambridgeshire, started a round. He first came to minister to Ashdon's sick on an old bicycle, then, not to be outdone by 'they posh owd quacks from Bunkum (Saffron Walden)', he bought a pony trap. Soon he opened a surgery in Ashdon in a room behind the bar of the Rose and Crown, taking a partner, Dr Gill, and attending twice weekly. Dr Palmer was conscientious and benevolent, and endeared himself to the old and ill, to most of whom a bedside manner had formerly been a mystery. 'A proper Christian' and 'a real genuine poor man's doctor, bor,' said the farm workers who flocked to his surgery. A second surgery was started at the White Horse, just over the Crown Hill, by Dr Thelwell of Saffron Walden, and when he died it came under the charge of Dr Hepworth, also of Saffron Walden. These two doctors came in new motor cars, all bright and beamy with acetylene headlamps. Dr Palmer hurled himself into the realms of internal combustion on a pop-popping motor bike. He was big physically, but his was a puny machine, and he looked somewhat lugubrious and disconsolate as the Saffron Waldeners overtook him in their shiny limousines.

Paying the doctor was a problem for farmhands, whose wages averaged 12s a week. It was worse after retirement age, for they received no pension before Lloyd George's National Insurance Act of 1911. 'If it worn't for the cost o' that owd elm box wi' brass handles, payin' for that owd hearse, undertaker, top hats, wreathes, parson an' the grave digger, I'd be better off a-dyin', bor. Nobody wants you after you've worked your guts out on the land.' But a local branch was formed of a benefit society, the Loyal Order of Ancient Shepherds. Lodge meetings were held in the club room of the Rose and Crown, and subscribing members were entitled to medical attention and a few shillings a week for a limited period. Dr Palmer was mainly responsible for treatment and did the clerical work.

When bluff Dr Gill returned to Ireland, Dr Palmer took a new partner, Dr Wilson, and bought a motor car, chauffeur driven. Nothing could have given Ashdon more pleasure than to see him being driven in style along the narrow country roads and lanes. But this splendour was short-lived, and from a travelling salesman came the story that he was about to retire. 'Oi reckon owd Palmer's bein' took over by one o' they owd Scotsmen, and now we'll have to pay for treatment in advance.' As usual, the news carrier was right. The practice was taken over by a competent and charming Scot, Dr A. M. Brown, who came to love Ashdon and was admired by all his patients. Chris knew Alec Brown well, and says a worthier candidate for wings and a halo never existed. He died some time ago, after retiring to Scotland to a new house which he named 'Ashdon'.

Ashdon has been fortunate in doctors, but some of the older

patients still cherish William Palmer's memory, not only because he used to write about our village in the *Cambridge Chronicle*, with his friend Cyril Fox. 'It's all owd pills an' pellets nowadays, an' I fair rattle as I walk arter gooin' to the surgery. Palmer's owd jollop were the stuff, bor. They owd pills ain't got half the power.'

Our country lanes and highways were coloured with characters; roadsters, tramps, vagabonds, minstrels, tallymen, craftsmen and gipsies – travelling by Shanks's pony. Few stayed in the village more than a day or two. Some sought employment for their arts and crafts, most were trying to scratch a precarious living as they ranged from one parish workhouse to the next, and were generally regarded with suspicion. From long experience we villagers knew that nomads would steal even from the poor, or use violence to get a few coppers, and we could ill afford to be robbed. Sometimes we gave food and pennies, and afterwards regretted it. Cunning signs would be chalked in secret on palings, to indicate to other vagrants that humanity lurked in our houses. Then all would call to cadge, implore or threaten. 'I ain't had a mite o' food since the day afore yesterday. Honest to God, missus.' We used to take them to the bakehouse to wash their feet, then give them bread and lard.

Gipsy Green, now farmland, was named for the gipsies who used to camp there when it was a barren area surrounding the infrequently-worked chalk quarry. A belt of blackthorn and elder bushes screen the chalk pit from the high road between Ashdon and the Camps, but there was always some sign of gipsies sheltering in this spot – the distinctive aroma of a log fire and its thin blue smoke rising was usually the first evidence of their arrival. It was an ideal camping site, with the necessary shelter, abundant firewood, a streamlet providing fresh water, and an abundance of rabbits in the quarry warrens. A hazel thicket across the road supplied wood for making clothes pegs, and round a bend in the road their shaggy ponies grazed on the rougher grass.

It was good to see the caravan of gipsies arriving. The bright vans wound leisurely along the country lanes, no two painted alike, and every surface covered with an endless variety of designs; a swarthy gipsy with forehead curls and ear-rings walked ahead of his pony, followed by his family. As his van passed, the half-open door at the back came into view, over which a wrinkled grandmother leant, enjoying her clay pipe, her 'swiggler', spitting tobacco juice and calling sharply to children and lurchers trailing behind.

Gipsies sold clothes-pegs and paper windmills, told fortunes and cast spells, all for sixpence. Pedlars carried trinkets, matches, boot-laces, studs, kerchiefs, pots and pans, and wooden boxes filled with dress lengths, shirt lengths, flannel nightgowns, Price's night lights, and all manner of crockery. Once they got a foot in the door they would not leave until they had made a sale. Buskers played on trumpets, accordions, tin whistles and trombones. The music was not up to much, but it was a pleasant diversion. Children preferred the hurdy-gurdy man, who turned his handle and churned out all kinds of tunes to set them dancing. Usually a monkey dressed in a red jacket and chained to the hurdy-gurdy danced and grimaced and showed its teeth as it proffered the collection. Cheap Jacks told long stories and sold tea sets, dinner sets, basins and hand-painted chamber pots.

The tinker we liked best had pushed his barrow into almost every nook and cranny of East Anglia. 'Joey Smith I were christened, but yew jest call me Joe.'

He was honest in his dealings, and trusted by the folk of the hamlet. Twice a year he made his headquarters in an old chalk pit, close to Camps Hall Farm and hidden from the road by trees and undergrowth. He was a lone wolf and in his hideout he built a semi-permanent hut which he repaired each year. This was his home during his tour of Ashdon, Bartlow, Shudy Camps, Helions Bumpstead and Castle Camps Endway.

We did not plague Joe as we did the unkempt vagrants. He came from Soham, Cambridgeshire and used to work his way there every few months to replenish his stock and clothing. He was always dressed in dark brown corduroy, and looked well washed. He was extremely tough and never ailed, although he was out in all weathers often wind-blown and half frozen. 'Oi jest gets a-gooin' on th' road. Th' owd barrer soon warms me up ag'in, bor.'

He would take up his stand at Bartlow Hamlet's cluster of cottages where we both lived and shout, 'Kittles ter mend. Kittles ter mend. Knoives ter groind an' kittles ter mend!'

Doors would open as though by some master switch. We would rush to him with spoutless teapots and kettles, punctured pans, useless umbrellas, blunted scissors, knives and billhooks. He would greet us all by name, for he knew most of the children throughout his wide area, taking a tally of who owned which. We watched with lively interest as he turned up his barrow on its short legs and carefully fixed the leather belt to the driving wheel, and we laughed and clapped as the sparks flew in fiery stream. He pedalled away, turning a blade from side to side, eyeing it critically and trying its edge for sharpness with a big, bent, blackened thumb. He sat on a folding seat as he treadled, humming or whistling a tuneless air, the happiest of men.

Joe never lost his temper. He did not swear like the tramps, nor did he ever charge more than twopence for sharpening any tool, even after renewing worn scissor rivets and giving the blades and handles a polish. Pots, pans and kettles requiring soldering had to be taken to his hideaway hut; but they were handed over in the sure knowledge that they would be returned the next day. Umbrellas were a speciality of his. They often came to grief, ribs were broken in high winds; ferrules wore down on the flint-capped road, and handles came off. Sometimes Joe fashioned an umbrella from his 'owd bits an' pieces' and sold it for sixpence.

An old chair-mender used to shuffle through the hamlet with a bundle of split canes tied to the side of a broken-down perambulator in which reposed the whole of his worldly goods. He died in a ditch.

Another old man would call at cottages to set and whet saws, a preliminary to wetting his whistle at the Bonnett Inn. He had a tremendous appetite for strong ale, and it was common to see him with his portable saw vice set up by the front wall of the Rose and Crown. He would rasp away at a furious lick at some householder's firewood saw, making a noise which set other teeth on edge, but the moment he collected his fee he would dash into the tap room and down a quart – for fourpence.

Teams of itinerant sawyers called at farms to work at saw-pits, and travelling bricklayers plodded through with worn-out trowels protruding from ragged pockets. Some were excellent craftsmen, but they were mostly of ill repute, working from one village to the next, drinking away what little money they earned; sleeping rough and scrounging food until necessity obliged them to move on. Some told tragic tales of their misfortunes; wives had died, farmers had evicted them from tied cottages, tools were stolen, illness overtook them and gipsies had fired their houses. Some brought children with them, who begged crusts from cottagers, and stole swedes and turnips from the fields.

Apart from pedlars, there were packmen. The large packs strapped to their backs contained boxes with ornate cards of collar studs, shirt buttons, needles, pins and 'waxed ends' – long lengths of stout thread with hog's bristle needles attached to both ends used by amateur cobblers for stitching leather.

Charlie Pettit called once a week with his covered wagon. He was a purveyor of paraffin, but his cart was also crammed with soap, cakes of brickdust and whiting, metal polish, dust-pans and other tin goods, and brushes and brooms. He reeked of oil and soap, always gave the children a ride in his wagon, and once filled a housewife's vinegar jar with paraffin. Charlie was a dandy in a greenish bowler hat, morning coat, wing collar and cravat, and a rose in his buttonhole.

Another man brought boxes of Yarmouth bloaters and herrings threaded by the gills on a long stick.

The workhouses were called locally the 'grubbies'. Sometimes whole families of repulsive-looking wretches processed through Ashdon from Kedington Workhouse, on their way to Saffron Walden Workhouse in the opposite direction. Children were urged not to go out on the roads on Grubby days, but the parental plea was superfluous. One look was a sufficient deterrent. Happily, due to the Vagrancy Acts, no such cavalcades are seen on our roads today.

11

Some eccentrics

When he wor at school th' boy Lubber wor slow;
  They culled him 'owd Hodmedod' ther, as Oi know.
    Of all o' thim stories, thet Parson once brought us,
      He on'y remembered 'The Hare an' the Tortuss'.

He got away loight wen things hed tew be done,
  Loiker garden tew dig, or a message tew run.
    The master he say: 'Ut's no use tellin' him;
      He'll be harfen hour afore he begin.'

Wen owd Farmer Cook at his Watersoide Farm,
  Went in fer a tractor, an' put in his barn,
    Young Lubber he say; 'That'll dew me a treat,
      All Oi gotter dew is tew set on th' seat.'

Soo he reads abowt 'ingines' along of a book,
  Thin he put his best hat on an' sin Mr Cook;
    An' th' Lard on'y know what young Lubber dud say,
      But he's droivin' that tractor tew this very day.

Hodmedod (snail) WILLIAM F. DOOLEY (1906–)

John **Purkis** kept one of Ashdon's two general stores. His little shop, close by the Baptist chapel, was dilapidated. He lived there with his sister Nellie. He was a wiry, robust little man who never seemed to have emerged from the Victorian era. His everyday clothes had a rusty, outdated look, like their wearer, and had long seen better times. In late spring and summer he sported a mothy-looking straw boater, its band faded to a rusty green. On Sundays and in winter he always wore a bowler. His 'hard hat', as he called it, was not as shabby as his boater, or as his everyday hard hat, and he looked quite jaunty as he made his trips to church, twice each Sunday, to blow the organ for Mabel Eason.

John's father who kept the shop before him had had a lackadaisical outlook on life which was quickly absorbed by

153

his son. Time meant nothing to John. Hurry and bustle were foreign words. He – the shopkeeper – was important and ordinary mortals had to realise that in serving their needs, thought was required, most leisurely thought. Nellie stayed in the living room until there was more than one customer; then she would emerge with a look of mild disdain, and an air of faded gentility. Her surroundings belied her beliefs.

The shop was dismal, and had not been decorated for years. Paintwork had dulled and peeled. The once white ceiling was almost as brown as the fixtures lining the walls. American cloth covering the two counter tops was worn away and exposed the shrunken boards in their uneven jointing. Facing panels were kept together by some hammer-bruised strips of tin – advertising Mazawattee tea – which were nailed across them. The floorboards between the two counters were badly worn and nails projected dangerously above the surface; as one walked across the shop the boards heaved and squeaked like screech owls. The glass of the entrance door was badly fitted and wind whistled through the gaps. Hinges caused the door to sag and grind out a protest on the wooden sill. Brute force had to be used to gain entry. Perhaps it was just as well, for the bell gave out a reluctant ping which could only be heard by those with acute hearing.

The two large windows either side of the door showed more bare wood than paint; putty crumbled from the frames and rain seeped through. 'Fry's Cocoa' in faded capitals glared from one window and under each, fixed to the brickwork, were two more tinny advertisements for Mazawattee tea. In the cast-iron fence enclosing a tiny front garden, an iron gate hung awry on its hinges, from which a path led to a small door opening on a flight of brick steps to the cellar, 'my warehouse', as John had it.

In this small subterannean chamber, lit only by a small pane of glass in the door, John kept his cheeses, tubs of imported butter and sides of bacon. On the far side a door opened into a narrow store room filled with wooden bins containing sugar

and blocks of salt alongside a tank of paraffin. A large Tate &
Lyle sugar box held a store of whiting balls used for whitening
hearths or whitewashing walls and ceilings. Patent distemper
was too expensive for the villagers and was distrusted.

There were two departments in the shop. On the right was
the grocery, as the fixtures on the wall testified. The counter
bristled with glass jars of boiled sweets, black jacks, humbugs,
pear-drops, aniseed balls, raspberry drops, acid drops, pepper-
mints and chlorodyne lozenges. Behind them, an array of
biscuit tins, ginger nuts, Social biscuits, dry crackers, fig rolls,
Garibaldis and, most popular with the children, penny packets
of coated and highly decorated biscuits with sugary icing. Wise
to John's ways, the children asked for a 'taster biscuit'. They
would sample several and then settle for a penny packet, much
to his annoyance. The same procedure was adopted in the
selection of sweets, and John often declared that he 'lorst all
his profit' on sweets and biscuits.

All goods had to be weighed out of stock. Sugar, in blue
paper cones, tea and coffee in white cones, and butter and
cheese in white paper bags. Alongside the antiquated scales
were weights ranging from half an ounce to one stone. Johnny
would select them very slowly, like a chess champion carefully
considering his next move.

From ceiling hooks hung an assortment of tin wares –
kettles, baking tins, saucepans – alongside hand-brushes,
broom-heads, distemper brushes; all showing signs of having
hung there a long time. Blocks of Sunlight soap were stacked
next to blocks of Lifebuoy, above a nest of drawers, labelled
nutmeg, spices, cloves, caraway seeds, chillies, etc. Larger
drawers contained currants, sultanas, plums.

On the drapery side hung an array of gaily coloured pina-
fores, voluminous women's garments of various sizes and
patterns. John always wore a white apron which he draped
around him like a shroud and secured with a great brass
fastener, more of a brooch than a pin, a bit like horse-brass
badges, but heart-shaped and highly conspicuous. John was

very fond of this fastener and would fondle it as he kicked the heavy fringe of his huge apron to allow him to proceed across the shop.

The drapery business had become too much of a burden for John, so he had engaged one Joe Lofts as an assistant. Joe was quiet and seldom smiled. He too wore a brass fastener on his apron, which invariably fell off as he mounted his little ladder to reach the shelves bulging with rolls of unbleached calico, flannelette and boldly striped shirting; the latter found a steady sale, for all the farmhands' shirts were made from this hard wearing and warm material. Joe coped with elastic, tapes, cotton and needles, darning wool, thick woollen or cashmere socks and stockings, cloth caps and the strong leather gloves worn by hedgers and ditchers; strong working trousers, most of them corduroy with great flap-fronted flies, and with sturdy tipped and hobnailed boots which hung on hooks over the counter. Children as well as adults wore these clodhoppers . . . 'Yew can git any size at Purkis's,' they would say. Joe's was the working man's emporium and most folk preferred to do business with him, because with a great show of competence and concern he would laboriously write out a specially worded 'urgent' order for anything out of stock. It was impressive to watch him moistening the nib as a preliminary, sometimes absent-mindedly popping the ink-filled nib in his mouth. But there was a reason why some customers preferred John to Joe. John would give credit . . . 'Pay when ye can, m'dear'. Joe always insisted on cash. Thus the drapery side prospered more than the grocery.

It was edifying to watch John dealing with a customer.

'Mornin', nice day!' His big smile seemed to sprout from the depths of his walrus-like moustache. With hands clasped behind him he would rub his backside, then walk away as if he had no interest in the business. Suddenly it would dawn on him that a customer was in his shop, and he would start all over again. 'Mornin', Miss Bird, nice day, but a bit cowd, like. What can I git ye?'

'Mornin', Mr Pukkis. Cheese, 'bout quarter pownd. Yes, the wind's cowd, but I don't like the cowd.'

'I ain't got no hot cheese, m'dear, yew want it mild?'

'I meant the weather, not the cheese. Father likes it tasty.'

'Huh, we don't seem to've got only mild out here, I'll hev to goo to the warehouse.' He mooched off to the cellar, key in hand. A good ten minutes later he returned, cheese in one hand, key in the other. As he neared Miss Bird he put the cheese to his nose and sniffed, then held it under her nose.

'Will that be strong enough, then? It's the hottest an' ripest I got.'

He picked up the cheese, sniffed it again, placed it on the scales and began to wrap it in white paper. When he picked up a sheet of newspaper for an outer wrapping an article caught his eye. Completely disregarding Miss Bird, he read the article through and began to comment on it. He then came back to reality, gave the cheese another sniff and said; 'No, we don't sell mucher this. Tuppence ha'penny.'

The coins were handed over. Perhaps half an hour had been spent in selling a quarter of a pound of cheese.

Each Saturday John would harness his old pony to the trade cart and 'do the rounds'. He had only six customers on the round, all in Radwinter, and he had only six parcels in his cart. Yet he departed at nine in the morning to travel the three miles, and never returned before six in the evening, and always paid a lad one shilling to accompany him. On his rounds John smoked a pipe (he never smoked in his shop). As soon as the pony was facing the direction of Radwinter he would begin, rubbing in his hands his favourite flake tobacco, Golden Honeydew, which had an exquisite aroma, so different from the harsh shag and plug favoured by the farmhands. There was no other traffic, so John would loop the reins over a cart hook by his side and allow the pony to guide him to his customers. About a mile from the village he would draw the old pony to the roadside, and whilst it grazed contentedly John would dismount and spend several minutes at the back of his cart. He had a bladder weakness. At each of his six calls John would drink a couple of cups of tea according to the local custom, and then at Radwinter's Red Lion inn he called for a pint or two to help down his luncheon sandwiches, so the rest of the journey can best be left to the imagination. On the homeward journey John was able to resume his pipe and finish off that first filling of Golden Honeydew. The last three calls were in the village, and they took up the rest of the day. As he pulled up at his old shop the school clock would be striking six, and Nellie would come to the door with her usual greeting . . .

'I'm glad yew'r' home, John. Yew must be fair wore owt, bein' away all day.'

The redoubtable Joe left to run a shop of his own in a neighbouring parish. John and Nellie carried on alone for several more years. But in 1921 mounting debts at last forced them to quit the old shop and they went to live in one of Ashdon's first council houses. Nellie married William Allgood, a soldier returned from Mesopotamia. John, who was a part of Ashdon, was left on his own. His idiosyncrasies endeared him to us.

Mike Wilson lived in the tiniest of cottages, its plastered walls and corrugated pinkish-brown tiled roof sheltered by tall larches which grew in the spinney half way up Church Hill. A burly figure in corduroys, Mike was slow of speech and wit, and slightly round shouldered, which he attributed to stooping to avoid hitting his balding head on the low ceilings and doorways.

His wife was affectionately known as Polly Mike. This was an apt name. Short, buxom and protective, she made up for the deficiences of her slower witted spouse, and was described as 'fierce as a flea'. They were inseparable. Their cottage stood in a narrow strip of garden. In one corner under the ancient sprawling branches of a decrepit apple tree, set close to the trickling ditch, was the privy. The tree seldom bore fruit. As

Mike often said, 'It's got owd, like me, full o' pests an' canker.'

Behind the cottage was a ramshackle pigsty he had made years before, which seldom lacked an occupant. He prided himself on his fat pigs, indeed he lived for them. The brine tub in the little scullery was never without a leg of fat pork for Mike, from which Polly Mike cut slices to boil or fry, as the fancy took him. From a hook on the wide chimney piece a pink ham in a muslin bag hung maturing in the smoke of the wood fire. 'It's a-dryin' owt,' Mike said. Although he had only a few pegs of teeth he managed to masticate lumps of fat pork plentifully daubed with mustard, and slices of Polly Mike's cottage loaves, washed down with the dark strong ale of his own brew.

He was a simple soul, with the simplest of tastes. After a partnership of sixty years Polly Mike anticipated his every whim. In his undemonstrative way he worshipped her, and called her Owd Owly, on account of her large round gold-rimmed spectacles. 'She look jest like a bluddy owd owl oo they grut spectacles on.' This was an endearing term and Polly Mike would smile indulgently, and sometimes blush. She knew her Mike and loved him.

Each morning at the old gate she had watched him going off to work, standing there until he turned the bend on the hill where great oaks overhung the road, and the moment she heard the click of the gate latch, or the tread of his big feet on the cobbled path, she went out to greet him. His meals were always ready the moment he arrived, and she waited on his every need. He was illiterate and depended on her entirely to eke out his wages. Polly Mike was capable, thrifty and even managed to save, but she took no credit, attributing her success to Mike's care of the fat pigs and his allotment just across the Ashdon-Saffron Walden road.

Unlike farmers' pigs, Mike's did not get a diet of skimmed milk, boiled and mashed 'pig-taters', nor meal, mash and root crops. Scraps from the vegetable pot partly fed them, and it was Polly Mike who paid for the pollard to mix with the swill, and she who bought the maize for the half-dozen hens penned behind the pigsty. Business was her responsibility. Mike was content to perform the menial tasks, cultivating the allotment, feeding and mucking out the pigs, and stacking the manure into a steaming mould which filled the air of Church Hill with its pungent odour.

Came the day when Mike decided it was time to see the butcher about slaughtering a fat pig. Leaning over the sty, calmly enjoying his clay pipe, he eyed the massive proportions of the Middle White as it cleared its feeding trough. He judged the time to be right, not only from the dimensions of the porker, but by the moon.

> Allus kill a pig when the moon's a-waxin',
> Never killun when she be wastin';
> Do, an' the pork'll be fit fer nowt,
> An' the fat'll waste oo the moon.

It was bright moonlight, and Mike knew the beams of a waxing moon were beneficial.

Sonny Pearson the village butcher and slaughterer lived a few yards down the hill, and a short walk confirmed that he was willing to kill the pig. Mike got out his mash tubs and set about stoking up the brick copper Polly Mike used for her weekly wash and he for his brewing. The water he fetched from the land drain over the hill in galvanised pails on his shoulder yoke. Polly Mike lent a hand scrubbing the inside of the mash tubs, then prepared her large earthenware pan for curing, and put ready the sugar, salt, beer and saltpetre. The killing was often carried out on the pig rearer's premises 'to catch all the blood to make black puddens', but Mike insisted on his pigs being killed way back behind the cottage, although it entailed more work. Sonny Pearson and Mike lifted the pig to the slaughter form, kicking, squealing, anticipating its end, and struggling to get free. As Sonny struck with his sharp knife there was a louder scream and blood spurted, but Sonny was an expert, it was a painless death and the pig was soon still and silent. Mike added his strength to Sonny's to swing the pig into boiling water and scrape the hair from its hide with comb-like knives, draw it, open it from throat to tail, and insert a stout stick across the belly-cut to keep it open. Then they hung the carcase from the branch of Mike's old apple tree. As always, Mike confided to Sonny, 'I allus hang the buggers there, cos there ain't a mossel o' room to hang em' inside, the ceilin' ain't high enough.' Sonny, who was well used to the procedure over the years of killing Mike's pigs, also knew exactly what Mike would do before he returned next day to dress and cut the carcase, set the different joints aside for Polly Mike to wrap in pieces of linen and muslin, and cart away all the pork left over.

Mike and Polly fed right royally on the liver of the pluck, and washed and cleaned the 'chitluns' as Mike called the chitterlings. Sometimes Polly Mike prepared them as gifts for her neighbours, immersing them in salt water and turning them each day until they were pink and ready for the pot, then she boiled then fried them till they were golden brown. Country folk all prized these chitterling suppers, and Mike's brother always came to collect his share and would depart to his home at the foot of Church Hill.

As darkness fell on the pig killing night, the ghostly outline of the carcase could be dimly seen as it hung from the apple tree. But none could see old Mike. Enveloped in a thick overcoat, squatting on the seat of his privy, he kept a sharp look out, his old single barrelled 12-bore muzzle-loader gun cradled across his knees, loaded with No. 4 shot, its hammer at full cock, the percussion firing cap in position. He watched the light go out as Polly Mike went to bed, the only time in their lives when she went to bed alone. He had only owls for company, their shrieks from the nearby spinney sometimes wakened him, and he could see his pig was safe.

Charlie Eagen was a native of Castle Camps, one perpetually haunted by problems. His long face betokened mental anguish, stomach disorders were but one of his troubles. He shared a cottage with his sister and her husband, with whom he did not get on – they hated each other – and that was another. There was no chimney sweep where they lived, and when the chimney smoked badly Charlie appealed to the constable.

'Whatever can we do? The whole house is filled with soot.'

'Get the bugger swept, then.'

'Can't afford it. They're owd, an' oi'm on the sick list.'

'Sweep it yerself, Charlie, bor.'

'Ain't got no sweeper.'

'Use mine.'

Next morning Charlie tapped on the back door of Police House, which was opened by the constable's wife.

'Oh, the brushes. In the garage, by the bench. Alec said don't forget to allus turn the rods to the right, else they might come undone. Best of luck!'

Charlie found rods and a circular brush, and barged into his sister's house, where the coconut matting had been rolled back and the furniture sheet-draped. He picked up a rod and began to screw it on the brush.

'Don't you oughter tie that on, tergither, then?' asked his sister.

'Corse not. She said all I hed to do was to keep a-turnin' to the right. Goo you down the garden an' holler when you see the brush fly out.'

The introduction into the flue of one brush and one screwed on rod brought down a shower of soot. Charlie ignored the mess. Screwing rod to rod he pushed them up the chimney, always turning to the right, even while pushing. An easing of effort coincided with a yell from the garden . . . 'Howd hard, you're through!'

Charlie wiped spectacles, brow, sweat and soot. A good couple of bushels of soot lay in the hearth. A shriek from his sister confirmed that a fair amount was soiling the protective sheets. He waved her away. 'Oi bluddy started, an' oi'll bluddy finish, even if I hev to suffer with me guts an' chest.'

Charlie was not the world's best engineer, but as he started his withdrawal exercise he calculated that if rods had to be screwed to the right to go up, it was only commonsense that they had to be screwed to the left to come down. As each rod descended it was unscrewed from its fellow, to the left, sometimes as it was descending. Then came the one to which the brush had been screwed. Charlie wiped his spectacles again, and glared. There was no brush. Much soot fell on him as he craned his neck to gaze up the swept chimney, hoping to see blue sky. He saw blackness. The brush had shut out all light, and was lodged.

'Is it clear, then?' asked his sister.

'No, the bloody brush hev got stuck.'

'Towd you to tie it on, di'nt I?'

'Oi'll soon knock it down, oo the rods. Bugger orf!'

Charlie screwed and pushed again. An hour later he had to admit defeat, the thread of the top rod declined to engage with the thread of the brush, clockwise or anti-clockwise. Brother-in-law Wag cackled in the parlour, revelling in Charlie's failure. 'Where you goin', Charlie?'

'Fetchin' a ladder.'

He borrowed one from the builders, climbed to the roof and precariously astride the ridge he peered down the chimney. The brush was beyond his reach.

'Can you see it?' asked Wag.

'Oi can, an' I could reach it if you'd hand me a clothes prop.'

'Come an git the bugger. You said you'd finish it, now's yer chance.'

Charlie climbed down, and up again with the prop. It just reached the brush, and he puggled away vigorously until the brush crashed to the hearth. A cry of alarm made Wag jump. Charlie was performing acrobatics on the roof and swaying backwards. The chimney pot toppled from the vertical and crashed to the ground, leaving a trail of broken tiles. Half stunned, Charlie lay on his back on the roof, then scrambled up and with all his strength hurled the prop to the ground. It hit the patch of concrete on the path and rebounded through the glass of the bedroom window. Wag was delighted.

'I reckon you 'on't finish, like you said, until you've paid the damages. It'll take years!'

Charlie's 'chimbley' was the talk of the village.

12

A postman's round

When martlets left the cobwebbed eaves,
And russet corn was bound in sheaves;
When sunflowers bent their aureoled heads,
And spiders spun their migrant threads;
When skies were poems ready writ,
And morning mists were infinite;
When berries dazed the insect throng,
And leaves fell through the robin's song;
Said I, the season passeth by,
My luck upon the road I'll try.

When winds were wild, and roofs untiled,
And coloured leaves in corners piled;
When bat and dormouse went to sleep,
And bough and sky did frequent weep;
When nuts were plucked and medlars sucked,
And pheasants shot, and furrows mucked;
When suns were dim and days were brief,
And winds re-howled their ancient grief;
Said I, the road now calleth me,
A Pilgrim once again I'll be.

When pool and stream were frozen hard,
And cattle stayed within the yard;
When elms were red, and ash-trees black,
And sparrows robbed the farmer's stack;
When tilth and farrow changed to stone,
And hoodies fought around a bone;
When hands were numb and minds depressed,
And snow the naked trees had dressed;
Said I, I will away from here
In this hard season of the year.

Yet here I stay, and years go by,
And Suffolk knows the reason why.

from *To Suffolk* CECIL LAY (1885–1956)

In 1916, when the war was in its third year, many Ashdon men
were fighting in Flanders, including Mr Newton our village

postman. During his absence Walt Symonds's wife became an auxiliary postwoman, and the few shillings that she earned delivering the mail while her husband was in the army were more than welcome. Charles Eason, the sub-postmaster, did not think she could manage the long walks across muddy fields at Christmas time. He was at his wits' end until he thought of asking Chris to come and be a temporary auxiliary postman. Chris, only fifteen at the time, was mightily pleased at the idea. His share of the round was to be over fields, along muddy tracks and long footpaths.

The first frosty morning he set off with his bulging post bag, the strap buckled to the last hole, but still bumping un-comfortably. On his right arm blazed the red and gold brassard which betokened a carrier of the Royal Mail. The heavy load lightened after working from door to door through Roger's End and Holden End. It became even lighter at Knox End, where more children were born than anywhere else in Ashdon. Their fathers sent them presents from wherever they were serving in France or even the East.

The bag still bumping, Chris's walk across country revived earlier memories. The old walnut tree stood like a sentinel near the chalk quarry. He and I used to throw sticks at its green husks; and it was once the shooting butt of the rifle club, sometimes described as the poachers' training school. Chris's brother Jack was captain of the team before he went to Flanders, and Chris would go with him to watch. They brought their own beer, rifles, sandwiches, and one brought a gramophone on which he always played military marches and love songs. They were all good poachers of partridge and pheasants. Many of them could even hit a woodcock on the wing, which with its tricky flight was a most difficult thing to do. My uncle Jasper Miller, the estate gamekeeper, was very put out by their good marksmanship.

From the walnut tree Chris went on to a pair of plastered cottages known as White House, then across the railway to a solitary bungalow to deliver a letter to another gamekeeper,

Stuart. Being a 'foreigner' as well as a gamekeeper, he was not held in very high regard. He may have been glad to get his letter from Scotland, but the click of the gate-latch brought the black Labrador barking and Chris received nothing but a frown from his owner.

As he turned towards the farms of Great Bowser and Little Bowser, the path lay over fields, almost to the parish of Hadstock. On the red road the going was rough with frozen ruts, solid ridges and ice-encrusted depressions made by the hooves of the Suffolk Punches, but the redness shone through. The road was built with broken bricks from the brickyard, which had been ground to powder by the passage of tumbrils and haywains.

Charlie Eason had said: 'Watch out for the three Bs, boy. Bulls, boars and billy-goats.' Chris met all of them and came to no harm. The cottages at Great Bowser were occupied by the families of two of his school friends, Chris Hagger and Jeffy Haylock. Jeffy's grandfather was said to be in Education, and perhaps he was in a way. He emptied the buckets from the school lavatories.

Chris's hobnailed boots clattered as he got on to the flinty way which led to Rickett's Farm, after which he reached the high arch of the railway bridge. There had been no station at Ashdon before 1910, only a level crossing at Fallowdon's Lane over the single-line track from Saffron Walden to Bartlow. When Captain J. A. Collins came to live at Ashdon Hall he approached the authorities of the Great Eastern Railway with a proposition for a platform near the level crossing. They agreed on condition that intending passengers subscribed £12 to the cost. The villagers were more interested in becoming passengers than subscribers; so Collins paid the cost himself and promised to purchase a first-class season ticket. The work was put in hand and thus Ashdon Halt came into being and Captain Collins became the village's first commuter. The station comprised a platform the length of a cricket pitch; two standard oil lamps with *Ashdon* painted on the inside of the glass;

and a shelter – a disused railway coach with wooden seats and a door window. In next to no time villagers who had declined the subscription were travelling to Audley End, Saffron Walden, or Bartlow, just for the ride. Four trains ran each weekday, just two old coaches pulled by a puffing tank engine. Those were pleasant sounds as it snorted and whistled round the leafy glades of Sheddal Wood.

On Chris went over the water-worn stones to the Rectory at Church End, where Tom Green, the groom and gardener, smiled and waved his hand. Half a mile further on he reached the village again, as the school clock struck nine. At the Post Office on Crown Hill the second batch of mail was ready.

As he made his way to the outlying farms of Winsey and Bourne, Chris was on familiar ground near his birthplace. His five brothers were in the army and he looked in his mailbag to see whether they had written before he stopped at the Ketteridge cottage. There were telegraph envelopes with bad tidings for others, and he did not want to deliver one of those to his mother. Her hands trembled as she eagerly opened her letters bearing the stamp of the field censor and the capital letters OAS. Then she would tell him the news over a quick cup of tea.

His next call was at Kate's Lane and Great Sandon's farm where we got our skimmed milk. Kindly Mrs Hill gave him two of her best brown eggs. Then it was field tracks all the way to Farmer Sheard at Winsey on the high plateau which extends into Castle Camps. There an enemy lay in wait; a billy-goat that was so aggressive that Chris made detours to avoid him. When he failed and the beast attacked, he threw one of his boots at him. Unfortunately the goat began to eat the boot and it was only finally retrieved by Chris hanging the mailbag over the goat's horns and thus over its eyes. The moment he took the bag away he received a good butt through a hole in the hedge.

The next quarter of a mile, to Bourne Farm, lay along a sheltered, well-wooded vale with five groves, Griggs's, Pig's

Foot, Bendysh, Helions and Steeple. It was here that the shepherd lived out with his flock during the lambing season, which was at this time of the year. He had a hut in the corner of a field and it was drawn on wheels from fold to fold. Within a fortnight 200 out of 300 ewes would lamb and the shepherd kept his clothes on for a week at a time.

Bourne Farm took its name from the River Bourne, which supplied water for drinking and washing on its course from Knox End to Water End, but after any heavy rain, owing to the mud the water had to be taken from galvanised storage buckets. Commonsense dictated boiling it, but many people used it as it was, and none seemed to suffer ill effects. People living a distance from the stream were more fortunate in the quality of water from the land drains, though the flow was sometimes reduced to a trickle and receptacles had to be left in catching positions. In the drought of 1921 the land drains and the Bourne both dried up, and cottagers, children as well as adults, trudged across country to springs and wells, laden with pails, saucepans, wicker-cased jars and milk flap-cans. People who lived too far from wells and springs relied on brackish pond water, and rain water caught in butts in springtime. But there was a taste to this water, even after boiling, and one could see water dragons and other life in one's tea.

Two pumps still stand in the village, one on Crown Hill, the other at the junction of the Camps road at Holden End. Church End has two wells, both provided with windlass and bucket, one at the junction where Faldon's Lane meets the Saffron Walden road, the other, a very deep shaft, in the yard at the rear of All Saints' Church. Most farmhouses had their own wells, and most of the public houses; but strangely enough Walton's Park had no well. Walton's supply was from a large pond in the rookery piped to a system of filter beds from which it was pumped to storage tanks on the top floor. Major Luddington drew his drinking water from a controlled spring behind his gardener's cottage, which never failed in the hottest weather and the longest droughts. The Ketteridge family had

169

a well in the grounds of Mill Cottage. Behind Reuben Ford's cottage was a meadow spring contained in a large brick chamber which was periodically opened and cleaned. It provided an inexhaustible supply of pure water to the nearby cottages in Bartlow Hamlet. My brother and I yoked pails to our shoulders and made our way to the communal tap, reached by crossing a narrow wooden bridge over a stream feeding Sparks's, where water flowed across the road and horses paused to drink on the Ashdon-Camps road. The tap has been removed, the bridge has rotted to ruin, but water still trickles through the old pipe to an ornamental rockery standing in the grounds of the keeper's cottage.

Sinking a well manually is an arduous and lengthy business. If sunk through chalk, there is often no need to line the shaft with brick, because firm chalk holds without danger of early collapse. But this is not the case if the shaft is sunk through clay, when a brick lining is essential.

A most ingenious method was employed by local well diggers, which ensured a perfectly circular brick lining, and at the same time protected the man working at the bottom of the shaft. A wooden cylinder was made to the dimensions of the shaft. This was hollow, 6 ft deep, and formed by nailing rough boards to a circular rib cage. This wooden curb was lowered into the shaft, the top resting just above ground level. Then course by course the whole cylinder was filled with bricks. All round the top of the projecting portion of the curb a layer of concrete was laid; this retained the shape in a perfect circle. As the digger below removed clay and earth from the centre of the well, the weight of bricks and curb followed him down, at the same time marking out the circumference. The helper above, who winched up the excavated soil, also laid successive courses of bricks as the curb gradually sank; thus by placing the bricks tightly to the edge of the concrete template the lining remained perfectly circular and the shaft truly vertical.

Although the bricks were laid without a mortar bond

between them, they were sufficiently firm to resist pressure from the sides of the shaft, and served at the same time to protect the excavator below from falling debris. The deeper the man worked the more he was helped by the weight of the bricks cutting into the soil, leaving him to concentrate on the central areas.

This method had several advantages; comparative safety for the digger, a truly vertical shaft, and when he had dug down to the spring, the satisfaction of finding it broached in full flow. When the well was lined to a depth of 40 ft or 50 ft, only the upper works remained to be completed. Doors were made to cover the mouth for safety. The carpenter would be at hand with wood, and iron hinges made by the blacksmith, to make a windlass, a rolling pin with iron cogs at each end and a turning handle. And there would be a cluster of delighted women, smiling and gossiping about the masterpiece which ensured them a constant supply of pure drinking water from a natural spring.

As Chris continued on his round, the hedgers and ditchers were out cutting dead wood, removing weeds, brambles, bellbine and the long tentacles of the wild rose. The sturdy young hedge-growth was left, partly cut through and layered back to thicken the hedge for seasons to come. Ditches were dug out so that land drains could flow freely. Thick poles were trimmed and stacked to sell to the hurdlers. Brushwood was bundled and tied in handy-sized faggots fastened with wythes made of nut hazel. These were for fire kindling, for firing brick baking-ovens, for making pea and bean sticks. The hedgers themselves got 'hedger's perks' or firewood. Brambles, rough scrub and the soft wood of hedge willow and elder were burnt, and in the waning light of wintry afternoons there were flame flickerings, smoke waftings, and that unforgettable aroma of roasting herbs, borne on the breeze, but lingering in the corduroys of the burner for days, and for ever in the minds of young countrymen. Ash grey patches long marked the site, and in their depths pheasants and partridge busily preened their feathers. Many a proud cock pheasant has come to an untimely end in its concern for cleanliness. Gin traps, mole traps, nooses and coppery snares were hidden in the ashes, and perhaps a brace or two of unsuspecting pheasant would grace an ill-stocked larder.

Walt Stalley was a highly skilled, industrious farmhand. An expert with scythe and hedging and ditching equipment, it was he, during the 1914–18 war who first dug the deep narrow trenches for Overhall Farm's land-drainpipes. With plough he drew a series of deep furrows where the trenches were to be dug, with shovel he cleared the earth, with spade he removed another spit a foot deep, and with grafting tool – a long-bladed spade tapering about 18 in from the tread – he removed the last spit of clay, cleaning up the bottom with a specially made hooked spoon on a long handle. With another long-handled hook he placed the earthenware pipes along the bottom of the trench, and covered them with whitethorn and blackthorn branches to prevent earth fouling them. A bachelor, he lived alone in his little home, still called 'Walt's Cottage'. Brassy Stalley, Ashdon's first land-drainer, worked for the Haggers for over fifty years and lost not one day's work.

The old men of the village used to say winter was death. On the contrary, that December on his postman's round,

Chris saw the grass was still growing and the landscape was full of colour. There were scudding clouds and muddy water churning in a lively stream, and small mammals and birds, usually hidden amongst the leaves of trees and hedgerows, darted to find food. Winter ploughing was in progress and greedy rooks followed the two horse teams. Yes, there was plenty of life in December.

13

How we amused ourselves

'Twas on the morn of sweet May Day,
When Nature painted all things gay;
Taught birds to sing and lambs to play,
And decked the meadows fair.
Young Jockey early in the morn
Arose and tripped it o'er the lawn.
His Sunday coat the youth put on,
For Jenny had vowed away to run
  With Jockey to the Fair.
  For Jenny had vowed away to run
  With Jockey to the Fair.

The cheerful Parish bells had rung;
With eager steps he trudged along,
Sweet flowery garlands round him hung
That shepherds used to wear.
He tapped the window; 'Haste, my dear,'
Jenny, impatient, cried, 'Who's there?'
' 'Tis I, my love and no one near...
Step gently down, you've nought to fear
  With Jockey to the Fair.
  Step gently down,
  You've nought to fear,
  With Jockey to the Fair.'

'My Dad am Maam are fast asleep,
My Brother's up and with his sheep,
And will you still your promise keep,
That I have heard you swear?'
Then Jockey did his vows renew...
He would be constant, would be true,
His word was pledged, away she flew
O'er cowslips tipped with sparkling dew,
  With Jockey to the Fair.
  O'er cowslips tipped
  With sparkling dew,
  With Jockey to the Fair.

With Jockey to the fair ANON. (n.d.)

Before the organised national benefit schemes got under way, our villagers' Slate Club ran for a number of years, its head-quarters at the Rose and Crown. Saddler and harnessmaker Albert Bassett was elected honorary secretary, and licensee George Adams, honorary treasurer. Each member contributed sixpence a week. On production of a medical certificate – and his club card to prove that he was not in arrears – he qualified for benefit at 10s a week for six weeks, after which his case came under review. At Christmas, the affairs of the club would be wound up and the funds shared equally between all members. It was unfortunate if a number of members fell ill in January as there would not be enough in the kitty to pay them all. Through the abuse of a minority who were determined to draw out more in benefit than they subscribed, the membership declined. Ashdon's club reopened from time to time and finally ceased.

Goose Club membership was for male and female, adult or child. No sickness benefits were ever paid for these were thrift or savings clubs, and most pubs had one. Usually the licensee became treasurer and banked the club's funds with the brewer. Contributions could be as little or as much as the members could afford from week to week. Just before Christmas each member withdrew the amount subscribed, minus a small percentage shared between treasurer and secretary. 'Share out' was a fine excuse for celebration by solvent members, who invariably made a night of it – much to the benefit of the treasurer. A voucher valued at one shilling – to be spent in the house – was included in each member's packet; this came from the interest on the money banked.

Few cottagers could save to buy clothing unless they joined a clothing club. These were run by the grocer, a farmer, or the squire's wife. Housewives paid a few coppers into them when they could afford to, and around Christmas time they would draw out their savings and go off to Saffron Walden, Haverhill or Cambridge, where they found wide selections in drapery shops and could spend their money to the best advantage. Those who did not subscribe to the clothing club put up with wares toted from door to door by tallymen, who insisted on regular weekly payments. They charmed or bullied housewives into making purchases on the 'never-never', but became downright abusive and offensive if the money was not forthcoming.

Membership of the Cork Club was limited to patrons of the Bonnett Inn. Landlord Fred Rawson introduced the idea to his customers and spoke of the fun (and funds) it had generated in his Derbyshire village when he was a youth. The object was to raise money for refreshments, liquid and solid, later in the year. There were no membership cards. Each new member paid sixpence for the Bonnett Cork Club badge, a crown stopper from a mineral water bottle. Funds were raised by challenges, all of which had to be made on the premises of the pub. Any member, upon production of his own badge, could challenge another to produce his. If he failed, the defaulter was fined sixpence. Sometimes a challenger was caught out by failing to produce his own cork, and he was fined one shilling for making a false challenge. If a member was caught with two corks on his person he was also fined one shilling, and the club funds soon grew. The extraordinary feature of this fining was that, although there was little money in the labourers' pockets, the fines would be paid without demur.

One of the best examples of club spirit was when a dozen members of the Cork Club arrived at the Bonnett to get a final drink. They had just returned from the coast on a char-à-banc trip. Seeing them in their Sunday best blue serge suits instead of working corduroys, landlord Rawson challenged the lot to produce their corks, and promptly raised another six shillings. It was the talk of the hamlet for days. 'The cunnin' owd varmint knew we worn't likely to goo cartin' corks to Clacton!' But they were not above using a bit of craft and guile themselves.

Bunk Thake, a lad of seventeen, was mentally slightly

retarded and, like many others just after the Kaiser's War, had no regular employment. Now and again he would get seasonal jobs. One day he had been threshing at Place Farm. His colleagues persuaded Bunk to go to the Bonnett for a gallon of beer. One of them picked up Bunk's cork. Jim Marsh challenged him. 'Got yer cork, Bunk, bor? Owd Rawson's bound to ax ye for it.' Bunk searched but failed to find it. 'Never mind, take my,' said Jim, and to the others, 'better give him yars as well, lads.' Bunk departed with a gallon jar bumping in the sack across his shoulders and eight crown stoppers jingling in his pocket.

'Mornin', Fred. Oi wanter gallon o' bitter for me mets.'

'Mornin', Arthur. Here's my cork, where's yourn?'

Bunk chuckled. 'Oi gotter hull handful, look!' He slapped down eight corks on the oak table and was promptly fined eight shillings for being in illegal possession, and another sixpence for failing to produce his own. He paid up, but had no money left.

'Carn't let me mets down,' said Bunk. 'Give the buggers a gallon o' water.'

'Git the cards, then, landlord. Me an' Jack'll see 'em round the board for a couple o' quarts!'

'Cards' were dominoes. The pubs had several boxes of them, with cribbage boards and pegs to mark the scores. Many an hour would be pleasantly passed to the clicking of the ivory cards, and to much ribaldry and pungent wit.

'Laying out' was the most popular and the simplest. Each player had only to match the first card with a similar number, and to give a knock on the table if he could not follow. For this the old cards were brought into use, ranging from double nine to double blank. The object was for two partners to rid themselves of all their cards before their opponents.

'Windmill' began with the laying down of a double six. From this centre all other cards had to be laid in the form of an 'x', to represent the sweeps of a windmill.

'Honest John' varied from district to district and from pub to pub, and many were the arguments and accusations about a player not conforming. 'I ain't havin' that, bor. He were playin' Cambridge fashion!'

'Fives and Threes' required a certain amount of arithmetic; simple calculations were often beyond labourers who had taken to the fields at the age of ten to twelve years. Each player was required to match up a numbered card in such a fashion that the total of the two ends was divisible by three or five. If, for example, there was a five at each end of the laid cards and the last player had matched up one end with a double five, he could score the maximum of fifteen points; fifteen being divisible by five threes and by three fives, he could then peg eight – five threes and three fives – on the cribbage board. It was customary to play twice round the board, the winning pair being those who first reached the last hole.

Apart from Nap and Banker and Cribbage, few card games were played in tap rooms, but in bar parlours farmers, travelling salesmen and tradesmen, of superior wealth and education, would play brag, pontoon and poker, for quite high stakes. Labourers preferred games calling for a sure eye and a steady hand – and low stakes; thus shove-ha'penny boards and skittle boards were in great demand.

'Ringing the Bull' was a great favourite of the elders. Suspended by a cord from the tap room ceiling was a heavy metal ring; the cord being just long enough to allow the ring to swing, reach and engage over a wall hook. Originally the hook was the horn of a bull, and from it derived the name of the game. The object was to swing the ring on the hook and score valuable points. Much practice attained momentum and accuracy, but the old exponents were experts and could accomplish this time and again with ease – if beer and bets were involved.

'Pitch and Toss' with halfpennies was popular but expensive. 'Nix and Bricks' was less expensive and more popular. Tap room floors were paved with bricks, or square pamments (paving stones) liberally sand sprinkled. First, the players would clear sand within the area of one pamment, or a number of bricks. Each of the team would in turn toss a handful of coins to the cleared section. Coins falling within the cleared area were retained by the thrower. Those falling outside, or straddling intersecting joints, would be gleefully collected by the opponent, who added them to his next throw. Great cunning would be used by spectators to persuade someone who had knocked back a few jars to take part in the game. If he was a bit 'far gone' he could not discriminate between copper and silver; and when the coins rolled well out of the cleared area cunning feet would be clamped hard on a 'mite o' siller', to buy the poor thrower a practice pint next day.

'Pitch Penny' was another game for the old ones who obtained much of their beer money by their prowess. A hole slightly larger than a penny was bored in the seat of the oak settle. Below the hole, on the underside of the seat, was fixed a box drawer fashion to catch the coins. In turn the players would pitch pennies through this hole. The throwing point was at the opposite side of the room, a distance of eight to ten feet. All coins that missed were forfeit. Only those that went through the hole were retained by the thrower. Great skill was required to get the coins through, but the old ones had practised for years, their accuracy was uncanny.

Dart boards did not enter village pubs until the Kaiser's War, although farmhands had become familiar with them in the booths and stalls of fairs and galas; it was the younger element who took to them at first. The elders considered it a dangerous game in the tap room.

But there was one game in which all loved to take part. Usually played at holiday times or on occasions of local celebration, 'Tip it' was entered into by all age groups and both sexes. Half a dozen a side was the usual team, and two teams would face each other across the tap room table. Teams could be reinforced if seating permitted, but if females were playing they were usually encouraged not to sit at the ends. Only the bit, a threepenny piece, was needed for the play. Each team appointed its caller, whose job it was to toss for the start and to pass the bit to and from his team mates.

At the caller's shout, 'Down, then!' his team would drop their hands and hide them from view beneath the table top. With a great show of passing and re-passing they would try to baffle their opponents as to the whereabouts of the bit. At the call, 'Up then,' they withdrew their hands and placed them in full view on the table top. In turn the members of the opposing team tried to locate the hand concealing the bit. If they were successful they took over the bit and the other team had to hazard a guess. This was the simplest game in the world, but the way it was played in the Bonnett made it the most hilarious. Shrieks of female laughter, and an occasional scream, testified that groping hands were not always searching for the bit, but it all added to the fun.

Some inns boasted a skittle alley, where matches were played against other teams and villages, and most had table skittle-boards, a game similar to ninepins.

Children played most of the games their forbears had played a century before, but there were few shop toys in the homes of labourers. Girls had wooden hoops and rag dolls, boys iron hoops and pocket knives. We cut our own bows and arrows, catapults and whistles. Nature supplied all the materials.

When early autumn winds blew down the first green husks from horse chestnut trees the glistening brown nuts were quickly extracted and examined. Only the finest and largest were drilled and strung for the ritual contests in school play-grounds, on the Crown Hill and in village roads. There was little traffic, only two motor cars, and no danger. There was no better implement for drilling holes through conkers than the stiletto-pointed horseshoe nail, begged, borrowed, but more often stolen from one of the two smithies. The conker was then threaded on stout string about 18 in long. One boy would hold out his conker and his opponent would strike with his. The object was to smash the nut of the holder. Baking the nuts, soaking them in brine or beer, and other devices, were believed to toughen them and make them virtually indestructible. Such measures were considered un-sporting, 'It ain't fair, he's got an' owd baked-un!' Few would play with one who employed such low tactics.

Except for those little black ones on button-up boots, buttons were valuable currency for schoolboys. 'Buttons' was even more popular than marbles, and had many staunch adherents in the various teams and sides. To be left out of the team because one lacked buttons was embarrassing and degrading. White mice, Albino rats, Belgian hares and pet rabbits – as well as pocket knives, whistles, pop-guns and pea-shooters – were often swapped or temporarily pawned for a few bits of bone with four holes in them. There were varia-tions of the game. The oldest, much played in Bartlow, was a throwing game; but Ashdon's boys preferred the wall pitching game. To begin the contest 'Bartler fashion', a boy would throw a number of buttons a distance of 12 ft to 16 ft with the object of landing them in a hole about 4 in in diameter. All buttons landing in the hole would score 'one'. Those failing to hole could be flicked in with the fingers, each flick also count-ing 'one'. The player who holed all his buttons with the fewest flicks was the winner, and confiscated the others' buttons. To begin the wall pitching version – Ashdon fashion – a boy would pitch a button against the school wall. All eyes would be watching as the button bounced from the wall and fell to the ground. A good pitcher could make it bounce a long way. The next player would then try to make his button land as near as possible to the first one. If by spreading his fingers he could span both, he would take them. If he could not, they would be left and his opponent would make another pitch. When a boy had exhausted his stock of buttons he was com-pelled to drop out of the game; but this position would not arise so long as he had buttons left on his clothing. Many a boy has returned home from school with his baggy homemade breeches held up with binder string; but within a week he would go off home with pockets filled with buttons and arms filled with pets. He had won enough of the former to redeem the latter. Fortune was ever fickle in the game of Buttons.

Most boys had one marble bag. The experts usually had two. One for 'they owd clays', the hard-baked clay marbles of one colour, and a larger bag for the glass alleys. Rolling, Knuckling, Dropping and Ringing, were four of the most popular marble games, played in the roads, lanes and school playground. Rolling demanded the least skill ('Tha's on'y fer infants!') and required the use of a school gutter drain, or a rut in a road or lane. The first player would roll his marble along the rut. The next player would roll his and try to hit the first.

Knuckling was a game of skill in which old men would often take part. A glass alley would be placed on the ground, then, from a distance of 12 ft to 14 ft, the players would kneel and knuckle on to three marbles towards the glass alley. For each strike they could demand a glass alley from the placer, who had put down the first marble.

Dropping had the same object and reward, but instead of kneeling and knuckling the striker would stand over the alley and drop a number of marbles on the marker. If they failed to hit, or rolled beyond a specified distance, the marbles would be forfeit.

Ringing, or Taw, was the oldest game. Players put down a number of marbles inside a chalked circle. In turn, they would kneel, as for knuckling, but would shoot off their marbles with cunning thumb-flicks; the object being to knock as many marbles out of the circle as possible.

Most cigarette manufacturers gave away cards in the packets. Some depicted wild flowers, animals, ships of the Royal Navy and the uniforms of the British army. One brand was much prized, for its packets contained silk cards of banners, flags and heraldic devices. These were of no use for games, but made silk cushions for the sofa. There was much swapping of cards to make up the series of 50 or 100. The two main games 'Guess' and 'Flick' were usually played at school. One player would briefly describe the picture and his opponent would have to guess the serial number. If the guess was correct the card was his; if he failed he had to forfeit a card. 'Flick' was more popular because more could play and more cards would be won. A card would be placed face downwards, at the foot of a wall, then from a distance of about 10 ft other players would flick their cards with the object of covering the card and winning it. If several cards remained uncovered, the first player to cover a card could continue to flick until he failed to cover a card. Sometimes he could win a dozen in one series of flicks.

Fivestones, Hare and Hound paperchases, and more boisterous, and sometimes dangerous when played on the concrete covered playground, pick-a-back wrestling, often resulted in cuts, bruises and abrasions. Tempers became frayed and fists flew, and almost every day there were bleeding noses and blackened eyes.

Most games were seasonal, according to the state of nature's materials. When hazel wands, or the willow, were sappy and springy, it needed only one boy to attend school with a homemade bow and arrows to start a craze for archery. A boy might trundle to school an iron hoop, and in no time at all the blacksmith would be pestered with requests for hoops. Some would guide their hoops with an iron hook fastened in a wooden handle; others would flog them along with blows from a short stick, but a forked stick was ideal for guiding and controlling the clanking ring of steel. Hoops, catapults and slings seemed always to be in vogue at the same time, and one was considered inferior if one did not possess the three. Catapults were expensive to buy, but simple to make. The financial outlay was for 2 ft of square gutta-percha, greyish-black rubber from Malaya. This, carefully bound to the upper ends of a forked wood stick cut from a hedge, and the other ends secured to a piece of soft leather – usually the tongue of an old boot – was a lethal weapon. Many a pheasant has met its end at the hands of a catapult marksman. Slings were cheaper to make, but required more skill in use. Two lengths of whipcord were fastened to a boot tongue to form a pocket in which the missile was placed. Sometimes marbles were used instead of stones. The sling was then swung vigorously round the slinger's head to gain the necessary momentum for the cast, then one cord was released and the stone was hurled towards the target with great force and accuracy.

Spinning tops made their appearance in fine weather, and the stony village street became alive with boys and girls, all energetically flogging away at the homemade tops with home-made whips. Mostly the tops were improvised from large cotton reels. The central hole would be plugged with a wooden pin and one end of the reel tapered to a point and finished off with a hobnail scrounged from Bob Matthews, the cobbler. There were various types in assorted, glaring colours, but the favourites were the tall slender ones with bulbous heads, aptly and universally known as 'window breakers'. These would be chalked on their tops with coloured crayons and as they spun gave out a rainbow effect. Peg tops were pear-shaped and usually set in motion with a length of twine indoors, as they needed a harder, smoother surface than our flinty village street.

Wintry weather brought other boisterous pastimes. Sliding on village ponds and horse-ponds was one of the highlights for both sexes. Few had skates, but in hobnailed boots they would glide over the frozen surfaces and the nail clusters would cut myriads of white streaks in the black ice, 'candles', we called them. Snow brought out many a homemade toboggan, shod with steel runners by the versatile blacksmith – sometimes for sixpence, often for nothing. Children would hurtle down the steep slopes of Hilly Meadow shrieking with glee, and some-times fear, just before they crashed through a ten-foot high hawthorn hedge which flanked the meadowside of the village stream. Many a casualty has limped home, bleeding from hawthorn spikes, clothes shredded and soaked in ice-cold water, to get a tanning from irate parents.

Fierce snowfights were inevitable. Boys from one of the village's many Ends would be snowballed home by a gang from another, who in turn would often fall foul of hard-packed snowballs from another End gang waiting for them in ambush. Strangely enough, all were the best of friends as they emerged from school, but the minute their feet touched the public highway conflict would erupt and snowballs fly in all directions. Now and again there would be a kind of truce and we would see the boys from another End leap-frogging the whole of their way home, often a distance of two or more miles; their steamy exhalations clouding the frosty air as they bounded over bent backs and yelled with glee in the wintry afternoons.

Homemade toys were legion, effective and ingenious. Whistles were made from the tenderest branches of willow and ash; pop-guns from the hollow-stemmed elder. Pea-shooters of elder, plus a steel-spring 'busk', stolen from mother's corsets. From the stems of sheep's parsley were made water squirts and syringes. The sap-filled, hollow stems of this green plant would be cut into half-inch lengths to form ammunition for a primitive gun. The gun was a pliant stick, pointed at one end. The 'bullet' would be stuck on the point. When the stick was pulled back and then released it would fly swiftly and accurately to the neck of the enemy. Intriguing wind instruments which gave out a blaring note were also made from parsley stalks. By making an incision in a six-inch length, and bending it a certain way while blowing down one end, various notes and tunes could be played – if one could stand the rank taste of the mouthpiece. When the parsley stalks had lost their sap and were seared and dead they were known as cixeys. From them ingenious water mills would be made that turned merrily over the surface of a ditch in spate. Invariably the 'miller' would go to his home wet-footed and wet-seated, but happy.

Bird-nesting in springtime was a great adventure. We climbed tall trees and tall, thick hedgerows, sometimes with the help of a length of cord round our waists. We never took more than one egg from the nest and then it was carefully blown and placed in boxwood strewn with sand or moss. There was a thrill in being able to jump the wider parts of the stream, and even in falling in if we misjudged the jump. Hunting and robbing bees of their honey had its own sweet rewards. If we stirred up a wasps' nest we would dash away in a frenzy, snatching up dock leaves to apply to the stings. There was the thrill of being chased by the angry gamekeepers after wandering through the game preserves in nesting season; and desperate dashes across fields and skulking in hedges and copses to outwit the village bobby, whose big red hands delivered the most stinging clouts to the ears of boys caught scrumping apples from a farmer's orchard or in the act of smoking cuttings of bellbine.

Girls kept to their spinning tops, walking on stilts; parading and dressing dolls and teddy bears; hop-scotch, 'touch', and rounders. But most of the activity centred round skipping to tune. 'Tinker, tailor, soldier, sailor; rich man, poor man, beggar man, thief'; 'Horse and carriage for my marriage, wheelbarrow, tumbril, pony-cart'; 'Silk, satin, cotton, rags'; and so on. Girls lined up for turns on the short rope, an individual effort of speed skipping, 'Salt, mustard, vinegar, pepper, *bump*'.

Boys and girls gathered wild flowers to press between the only two books in most households, the Bible and *Pilgrim's Progress*. Some had their own little garden plots and grew their favourite flowers to take to teacher and to enter for the various competitions.

There was no month that smelt so sweet or looked so gay as July. Our lanes and hedgerows were thick with wild blossom. From first crack of dawn and the dew damping of day, right through the day and well into the night under the yellow harvest moon, drifts of wonderful perfume stole into our noses from honeysuckle, sweet briar, wild roses, and the night scented stock. From cottage gardens great cabbage roses added their perfume to those of flowering shrubs. Throughout the year there was keenest rivalry to produce the best flower garden, and on the allotments the men would try to outdo each other in the production of the longest and straightest parsnip, the most bulbous onion, marrow, and the best fruit and vegetables. But the greatest event, was the July Annual Flower Show, when rivalry, pride, stealth and cunning reached their zenith.

'Estate gardeners never ought to be let take part. They got the advantage. Don't wuk on the land all day loike we. Got grut green housen, glass housen an' best dung from the yards. First prize'll bound to goo to Walton's again.'

Major and Mrs Pelly, who owned Walton's before 1916, always invited the full co-operation of their large domestic staff in this event and gave Park Mede to the village for that day. Wide expanses of short-cropped turf provided an arena for the sporting events. Towering elms, beautiful beeches and hardbeams (hornbeams) gave shade from the summer's sun, and erected beneath them was a large marquee and hosts of tents and stalls for sideshows and refreshments.

Throughout the late spring and early summer evenings, housewives tended flower beds and tried out new recipes for homemade wine, bottled fruit, crab-apple jelly, jams and pickles. The menfolk worked quietly and shyly and walked about in unusual silence – as if by some unguarded remark they might impart to a rival the secret of improving the dimensions of vegetables or the taste and potency of their home brewed ale. To win a prize for ale was the supreme achievement. Farmers' wives worked long in spotless dairies to bring forth their best butter and cheese; the finest batch of eggs, the neatest and sweetest combs of honey. Homemade bread, cakes, pies, tarts and sausage rolls were the specialities of farmhands' wives.

Well in advance of the fête, handbills printed by Hart's of Saffron Walden appeared at conspicuous points throughout the village and in neighbouring parishes. For a day or two before the show there would be anxious glances to the sky, at sunrises and sunsets; keen listening to the notes of the birds; careful observations of height and twists of flight. And in the evenings groups of men drifted towards Park Mede with three-pronged brushes and buckets of whitewash to mark out the tracks under the expert guidance of schoolmaster William Tuck, who knew a trick or two about geometry and dimensions of sporting tracks – though we had none on our concrete playground at school.

One farmer sent cartloads of timber to make frames for the events; a gibbet-like structure for 'tilting the bucket', stakes at corners of a dais to be roped off for 'black and white boxing'; a dais for the Saffron Walden Town Band to regale the crowds with lively dance tunes and marches. Tarpaulins, barrels, paper-filled hoops, tunnels of sacking and an assortment of wide- and narrow-runged ladders were placed in position for the obstacle race, a stout pole sunk into the ground and anointed with axle-grease to baffle the climbers of the greasy pole. Land-draining pipes were put down in readiness for one of the funniest events, 'the rat in the drain-pipe'; and at the farm, soaking overnight, a stout wagon rope, 'to toghten it up a mite for they owd tug-o'-war teams'. If the weather promised fair, the grass would be mown short on Park Mede for 'bowling for the pig', but this was usually held on the library lawn of the big house, where the grass was smooth and flat as a billiard table.

On the eve of the show, laden processions from the distant Ends of our straggling village carried exhibits to the large marquee, to hand to committee members who recorded names and addresses before scrutinising entries for trickery. All would be carefully tabulated and placed in position for the morning's judging.

When the day dawned in the dells of our pretty village along the small stream hovered a light blanket of mist, a positive harbinger of a fine day. As the sun rose the topmost tip of the windmill's sail was the first to catch the rays of golden light. Radiance soon spread over Langley Wood's wide acres and we heard another good sign, the dawn chorus. Birdsong rang out from that wood as it has done for centuries on good days. Wild honeysuckle and dew-soaked roses sweetened the air. Our village was awake to a day of promise.

Labourers were early astir and away to their farms. They had much to do this morning to complete essential tasks and make up for time they would spend at the fête in the afternoon. Those who could took the whole day off; but cattle had to be fed, cows milked, eggs collected, and horses groomed and put out to grass. Coveys of committee members came and went before breakfast, carrying chairs, trestle tables, cup, plates and saucers; from pubs came glasses, beer mugs and useful-looking barrels. Last, but not least, a tremendous tea-urn with a portable boiler.

At nine o'clock the judges arrived from Saffron Walden. With its exhibits already in place the marquee was handed over to the fruit, flower and vegetable experts, James Vert & Sons, seedsmen and market gardeners. They always completed their judging in record time and with great honesty. No one ever quarrelled about their decisions. It would not be possible. The minute they reached their verdicts they went hot-foot back to Saffron Walden and their precious seeds.

Schoolmaster Tuck stepped down from the Union Jack draped dais which would soon hold officials for opening the show and added additional hazards to the obstacle-race course. Wheelbarrow and prodding pole for 'tilt the bucket' were placed ready, a cask of water and pails alongside. Two poles were connected by a long cord on which were suspended apples for the bob-apple contest; receptacles filled with flour and soot were put in the appropriate corners of the boxing ring, with spongy gloves for the contestants to dip first in water, then in flour or soot according to their colour. Harness-maker Alby Bassett got into instant confusion when handed rolls of tickets to exchange for entrance fees. They streamed away in the light breeze like the ribbons of the maypole.

It was a sight for sore eyes when the women began to arrive, some in pony-traps and broughams, but most walking. All wore high-necked summery dresses which trailed on the turf. Wide-brimmed, be-ribboned and flower bedecked hats added gaiety to the scene, as did the delicate parasols. Cries rang out from children as a large wagonette drew up. Resplendent in uniforms of scarlet, blue and gold, the bandsmen arrived and began to take down their shining instruments. There was a cheer for thin Tom Lacey, who could never be seen behind his bass drum, and all waited for the music to start. Horse-drawn vehicles arrived from other parishes. Albert Free disgorged one wagonette load from Castle Camps and drove off quickly for another. Farmers' gigs and traps came in convoys. The pubs were open all day and some of the occupants had obviously made a call or two *en route*. Having unloaded their families they drove to Walton's stables where their horses were stabled for the day.

A sign with the broadest of arrows pointed towards an area screened by canvas strips draped round four poles. Inside were two galvanised buckets. This was partially hidden by bush-growth and long grass, but patrons could be recognised shoulder upwards at a glance. No one cared. Another notice told its own story.

DANCING – ON LIBRARY LAWN
(IN BARN IF WET)

The band struck up a lively air and played until all the officials were seated and someone rang a bell.

Flower show president Jarvis welcomed the crowd, introduced Mrs Brocklebank and invited her to open the show. Her speech was short and to the point and she was soon under escort by curates and farmers on a tour of the exhibits. The show was on!

It was all good fun. Schoolmaster Tuck marshalled his pupils for the events. 'Ready, steady, go!' and off they went, Tuck's eyes following them. Housewives took trays of tea and scones to the bandsmen. Children crowded round Mrs Dick's stall with pennies to spend, laughing and shrieking with delight each time a wired-on cork 'plopped' from the stone ginger-beer bottle, or one of their schoolmates coughed and spluttered through sucking too hard on the liquorice tube of a sherbet bag. Labourers who had taken the day off knocked back ale and made guesses about prize winners. Some were already known – wives had elbowed into the marquee and found out before the official announcements were made. Fuller Smith grinned as he turned to Nipper Marsh, 'Your taters wholly deserved a fust, Nipper, bor. Proper beauties. Carn't beat Sharp's Express! Never counted on gittin' a fust oo my marrer!'

Tom Duschene introduced two of the boxers.

'Ladies and gentlemen . . . on my right, in black, none other than the champion of Knox End, Jimmy Marsh!' Jimmy bowed and received an ovation. 'On my left, in white, another Ashdonian, Dumpty Harris!' The crowd roared. 'Three two-minute rounds and one minute rest.'

Jimmy and Dumpty dipped gloves into water, then into soot and flour, shook hands and tore into each other. Spectators became belly-sore with laughter as flour and soot bespattered those within range. At the end of the bout Tom Duschene made it a draw. It was just as well. To distinguish black from white was impossible. On his way to the dressing tent Jimmy noticed the wheelbarrow standing by the 'tilt the bucket' frame.

'Hop in, Dumpty. Grab a pole an' I'll give ye a bath. I know you ain't had one since larst year.' Dumpty got into the barrow with the pole at the ready and Jimmy raced with him between the posts, but Dumpty tilted the board to his own advantage. Jimmy gasped as he was deluged . . . 'Fill the bugger up ag'in an' I'll let you drive.' Dumpty obliged, charged between the posts, and received his damping.

The fun went on until middle evening when the last event was staged. Ashdon pulled Bartlow over the line three times in the tug of war. Now clean and fortified with ale, Jimmy and Dumpty were the last who bowled for the pig. Jimmy not only beat Dumpty, but with the highest score of the day won the pig. Later he drove it home in the wheelbarrow he and Dumpty had used to delight the crowd earlier in the day.

The Flower Show was as good as over. Reverend Smith called forth the winners one by one to receive their money prizes, the highest amount was half a crown. The president thanked all and sundry, shook hands and then made a signal to the bandmaster. First the evening hymn, then all stood statue still for 'God Save the King'. Bandsmen climbed into their wagonette and returned the waves from the children. Crowds surged through the gateway, and a hole in the brick and flint wall. Farmers' gigs and traps arrived to take their passengers to the pubs. Some prize winners took home their exhibits to show off a bit, but the bulk of flowers, fruit, vegetables, and all the cakes, butter, cheeses and preserves had already gone – to Saffron Walden Hospital.

14
Afterword

In 1914 Ashdon boasted five major farms and thirty small-holdings. Today most of the smallholdings have amalgamated with the farms to form larger units more suited to modern farming methods. Where once a dozen or more farm workers were needed on one medium-sized farm, now three or four men with the help of up-to-date machinery can manage a much larger one. There are no more fine Suffolk Punch horses to be seen and the young men continue to drift away from the land.

In recent years Saffron Walden has provided employment for men who were made redundant and had to change their way of life. Karl Engelmann's big nurseries swallowed up surplus labour from the farms. Between the wars and since the last war other industries in nearby towns have provided alternative jobs. Few men now work within their own parish. The fast expanding town of Haverhill in Suffolk and the large villages of Linton and Sawston in Cambridgeshire have claimed many men from Ashdon's fields. They learn new skills and reap financial rewards greater than were ever dreamed of at the turn of the century.

But Ashdon's hilly fields still produce bumper crops of golden grain. The village's working population is now comfortably accommodated in modern cottages, council houses or bungalows. There are left only a few of those picturesque thatched houses of timber, wattle and daub that once graced the Ends and Bartlow Hamlet. Some have disappeared into the ground through disrepair and neglect over the years; those that survive have been modernised, often in a way that takes little account of tradition.

The main changes in the village can be traced to the 1914–18 war when almost every family lost one of its members and when many of those who returned from the front were maimed. As the war continued the labour shortage became acute. Prisoners-of-war and children worked on the land and women were recruited to the Women's National Land Service Corps. When German U-boats began to cut Britain's food convoys it became essential to grow more food at home. Farmers were told to plough up pasture land to grow more cereals and roots. In August 1917 the Corn Production Act became law and guaranteed to farmers substantial minimum prices for wheat and oats. This brought about a brief period of agricultural prosperity. Unfortunately it came to a halt in 1921 when the act was virtually scrapped. It had already become clear that the much promised new Britain was not materialising. For Ashdon's returning heroes there were no jobs and no new homes. Men who had fought for the nation and old men who had toiled on our fields to feed the nation were themselves starving.

Children nearing school-leaving age were aware of their meagre prospects. Girls would go into domestic service at the squire's mansion, the Rectory or the large houses in the neighbourhood. The lucky ones might get jobs in London. We boys knew that our lives would be spent in long hours of drudgery as labourers on the wide, wet fields of the farms. Our education, elementary and extremely narrow, did not qualify us for much else; so we accepted the inevitable.

An Ashdonian of sixty years ago returning now to the village would hardly recognise it. Trees have been felled, new woods grown, hedgerows vanished, ditches filled. Fields have been bulldozed into vast farming areas, enlarging the chequer-board pattern of the landscape, and the old boundaries are present only in the contours. Pastures once alive with grazing sheep and cattle have been given to corn. Herbage and hay, the green meat which was scythed daily for horses, are gone with the acres of lucerne. Sanfoin, trefolian clover, vividly contrast-ing on the hillsides with linseed blue and deep yellow seas of flowering mustard, are seldom seen today. The orderly rows of root crops – mangold-wurzels, swedes, turnips – have given place to sugar beet, almost the only crop that still requires manual labour. When seed time and harvest are over the fields become almost deserted. There are no more labourers patiently and endlessly plodding behind horses. The strong tang of horse sweat, the creak of leather harness and the voice of the plough-man have been exchanged for the odour of diesel oil and the roar of tractor engines.

Farm buildings have undergone many transformations. Huge erections of concrete, steel and asbestos have been substituted for the traditional style. Thatched barns where labourers wielded their flails are fast disappearing, and thresh-ing floors – where the Horkey revellers feasted and danced – are stained with oil drippings from giant machines. Rickyards, once the inspiration for many an oil painting, are weed-infested and empty, and metal silos raise their bulk to the sky. Chickens used to roaming at will near the cornstacks are now confined in metal cages, or deep litter sheds. Modern methods of weed control have superseded hand-hoeing and the horse-shim. Tractors roar back and forth spraying toxic liquids, chemicals and pesticides, destroying not only ravaging insects but dainty moths and beautiful butterflies, and the song-birds that did the job as nature intended, and so much better.

Where the labourer used to trudge over flint-bound roads before plodding the muddy fields to work in the chill of early morning, his descendant sits cosily at the wheel of a car which takes him, usually, to a workshop in a neighbouring town.

The village street is a hazard to be negotiated with care, for nearly every household has a motor vehicle of some sort, and the motor-cycles and scooters of the young roar distractingly where we played as children in safety. How much easier it would have been for us if we could have spun our homemade tops on such smooth surfaces. The roadman's work is far lighter, there is no mud to be removed with his great mud-hoe, the mud banks he used to build up on the verges and keep trimmed and planted with flowers are now dealt with by a mechanical trimmer, and his besom broom like those we used to cut and fashion in Langley Wood is outmoded. There are no wayside flowers. Renewing a road surface today involves a fleet of lorries laden with asphalt to feed the monster 'Barber Greene' machine, and diesel-powered rollers.

The Bourne itself has been diverted in Knox End on the Bartlow road, where horses used to splash through the ford and a narrow footbridge bore pedestrians across; a concrete bridge is there now, but the old stream still meanders through the heart of the village.

Perhaps the most startling contrast is in the sky. Sixty years ago only birds flew, and silent clouds; but today there are vapour trails and the thunder of jet aircraft shatters the peace. Wild birds still sing, of course, but their notes are drowned.

Our village school is the same, though now it is called a primary school; one of the two general stores, Charles Eason's, and the old Rose and Crown public house are still there, though no native of Ashdon serves in them. Two other pubs have closed down, the Lamb and the Fox, but the three remaining are fully licensed and modernised. The Baptist chapel, Clarky Cooper's old thatched cottage, and All Saints' Church remain. Inside, the church used to be lit by candles, then paraffin lamps, but in 1954–5 electricity was installed, which now pumps and powers the organ, instead of forgetful Johnny Purkis with the hand bellows; and the organ too has been moved to a new position, exposing the north window of the chapel. There is underfloor heating in place of the slow-combustion stove which used to give out choking sulphur fumes and little heat. Roofs of the nave, chancel, side chapels and Lady Chapel have been de-plastered, revealing fine timbers, but the most ambitious act of restoration in All Saints has taken place in the old belfry, by the gift of Edmund Vestey, the present owner of Walton's Park.

New housing, privately owned or built by the RDC, is most substantially constructed in pleasing designs. The yard where Nipper Marsh and his brothers used to make hurdles is now an estate of new chalet-bungalows, and next door Nipper's old cottage was demolished to extend the Bricklayer's Arms car park. Around the corner by the Bonnett, new bungalows have sprung up like mushrooms overnight, a camping site occupies the field behind the inn, and in summer the grass is covered with coloured tents and caravans. Sleepy Bartlow Hamlet and Reuben's Corner are bounding with modern vitality, and the Ashdon dialect is often drowned by foreign tongues, for 'they owd furriners' come to the caravans, drink Greene, King's ales in the Bonnett, and follow the path over the fields to photograph our old windmill, half a mile away.

Farm workers can now get a respectable wage – huge compared with 1910 – and a paid holiday which was unknown then, when even Bank Holidays incurred a loss of wages.

There are other changes. I did not realise this until March 1971 when I went to Haverhill, Suffolk, to see my brother Leslie, just forty-seven years after I left Reuben's Corner. Fifty years ago our whole family went to Haverhill Gala, my father driving a pony trap. Women were gay there in their new summer finery, with flower-bedecked hats. They travelled to the show from neighbouring villages in gigs, broughams, wagonettes, dog-carts, and on Shanks's pony. Candy-striped in reds, yellows, blues and greens, and shining in the strong light, huge gas-filled balloons strained on white-washed tethering ropes; their wicker baskets filled with men and women in gay caps and silky blouses, and sacks of sand ballast, all ready to take off for the big race. There were hurdy-gurdies, swings, tinkers, roundabouts, clowns, coconut shies, hoop-la and hokey-pokey stalls, and bright brass bands. Horses and ponies were spruce, satin-coated and split-plait braided in rye straw in mane and tail, and with crinkly rosettes on the brow-bands and jowl studs of head-collars, all ready for the judging. There was long, lush daisy and buttercup studded grass, high hedges, higher spirits, music and laughter. And then, long after the sun had gone down and the naphtha flares took over, and we had left the gala seven miles behind, just before we turned Reuben's Corner for our brick and flint cottage home, I heard the roundabouts singing in the wind. I shall never forget that tune, and certainly not the words; for when I sang my choirboy version to her, just to show off, Mother told me to moderate my language and landed me a hefty clout on the ear. I still like the words . . .

> Oh, oh, oh, my sweet Hortense,
> Got hairs on her belly like a barb wire fence.

So in March 1971 I tried to recapture the poverty, richness and vitality of my childhood, by walking from Haverhill to Reuben's Corner, Ashdon; retracing my mother's steps before the Kaiser's War, when we were half-starved, and she pushed my brother Leslie and my sister Poppy in the old pram, with me walking, to Auntie Harriett's funeral. It came back so vividly.

The barn under whose thatch we had sheltered from the jersey-soaking thunderstorm looked mothy and slatternly of thatch. There were still white-painted posts and rails at the bottom of long, steep Whiten's Mere Hill, where we stole and ate a swede from a farmer's field because we had no other food. Shudy Camps Church was locked, bolted, chained and barred, as if the stench from the new battery pig farm was trying forcibly to enter where humans had ceased to go. But in the small copse at the road junction Shudy Camps–Castle Camps was an unusual shrub. Half a century ago my cousin Charles

Ford had amused himself while waiting each morning for a tumbril cart to take him to work, by trimming the blackthorn in the shape of a fox terrier; just snipping a few thorny twigs each morning with his sharp shut-knife, down all the years. I was delighted to see his shrub had escaped the crocodile teeth of those rapacious electric saws which hacked all the life-bearing hedges to the ground, leaving the fields exposed to that wind which blows so keenly from the Urals.

There were no Suffolk Punches, no pony traps. I counted eighty-five motor cars on that nine miles of country road, whose drivers neither waved, spoke, smiled nor offered a lift; not that I needed the latter. Two rabbits had been ground into the road by whirling rubber-shod wheels; one buck, one doe, two-year-olds; and one missel-thrush. Only one pair of human feet other than mine were on those roads, although I met three people not in motor cars: at Nosterfield End, two young girls, one seated on her pony, the other on the seat of her bicycle, her hand in the pony's mane for towing. I wished them good afternoon, then told the dark-haired rider to press her knees more tightly to the saddle flaps, keep her toes up and her heels down, her legs well behind the girth, and to ease and feel the reins with her thumbs up for good luck. She told me her pony's name, said I knew about horses and riding, and was my tie the Pony Club tie. I said it was, in a way. It was the tie of the Blues and Royals. 'Have they a club in Saffron Walden, then?'

The other pair of feet was only spasmodically on the road, and belonged to the new London landlord of our old Bonnett Inn, who did not know where I could get a cup of tea in my village. I watched him being hurled most uncomfortably on a semi-airborne walk by his great dog.

Walking round Reuben's Corner to Brick and Stone Villa brought throat lumpiness. Granny Fords' and OURS had been knocked into one cottage with a new name, Brick and Flint Cottage. Not a sign of mud under the eaves. And the house-martins, swifts and swallows used to come to us every summer.

Perhaps the insecticides and herbicides had killed the insects and flies they fed on, or perhaps killed our birds, before they could hatch their eggs. The old mill stood across the two meadows, but where my father had his wonderful garden there now stands an ultra modern bungalow, with all mod. cons and a garage whose doors fold like Neapolitan blinds at the touch of an electric switch. And on the ground from whence towered the trees of our harvest apple, the Golden Noble, and the William pear, there is concrete. Spring water still trickles through the land-drainpipe, but no one catches it any more for drinking.

Then on past Place Farm, whose fields I had worked upon in all weathers; to the grass verge by the huge barn where Poddy Coote and Barney Bland and I used to mix the cattle bait. On, past Walton's Park, the squire's mansion, where I started work at ten as a boot boy, and cleaned knives and poultry, and fetched kindling and drinking water in the dog-cart. There was no one about, not a flower in the verges, and we used to see violets and primroses in late March. The hedges of Holden, Thruskells and many other fields were gone. The five-barred gate down New Road Hill, where I told my schoolgirl sweetheart Nellie that I was going away from her to be a soldier in 1924, was just on its hinges, but could not be swung as we used to swing on it, for rust.

'Come yew on in, Ced. Hev a drop o' dandelion!'

Gordon (General) Goodwin was waving from the window of his new council house. He knew my footsteps. His wife Hilda looked concerned. General had just emerged from Addenbrooke's Hospital, Cambridge, after drastic surgery.

'They tell me I shan't wuk ag'in, Ced . . . Drop more? Done me bloody share, as well yew know.'

We used to work together, on the fields.

'Tell me, General, how you learned to know everyone in the village by their footsteps.' I reminded him of that dark night when I walked up New Road Hill for the first time in nine years, after serving two years in Egypt and five in India.

And in that blackness, when I could not see a hand in front of my face, a voice rang out. It was General's. 'Goodnight, Ced. Spect yewv'e got some leave, then.'

General chuckled and winked broadly at Hilda. 'Easy, when yew hev tew! It were like this. We were a-livin' in Collier Row. Times were bloody hard. All them kids, an' mother never let none on us hev a mite o' vittles arter arternoon school till father got home from wuk. "Yar father goos owt to arn the money tew git the food. He's the fust t'be fed. Yew'll hev to wait, the lot o' ye."

'Well, Ced, bor, we were that bloody famished, we uster set by the front door a-listenin' fer father's steps. We larned lots o' the tothers. Couldn't stop listenin' arter that.'

And then I walked to Collier Row. Mrs Smith was pleased to see me. She used to live next to Mother after Granny Ford died, and was a firm friend. I wanted to see the graves, and asked, if I raced up Church Hill would I be in time for Evensong?

'Evensong, Ced, boy! They don't hev that no more. Arternoon services now. Parson'll soon be knockin' that on the head, I reckon. On'y three turned up larst week!'

In the Rose and Crown yard Christopher's 1919 mortar-mixing shed had been turned into a garage. The Loyal Order of Ancient Shepherds' club room-cum-Dr Palmer's surgery, was now a well-appointed dining room with an extensive and expensive menu. The new ex-Grenadier landlord proudly showed me his improvement. He had not replaced oak with plastic and formica, but had painstakingly removed two hundred years' papers and thick varnishes to disclose old tapestries and fine carvings in the original oak. He told me Sheddal Wood had been conveyed to the trust of the Essex Naturalists in 1969 to protect the beautiful East Anglian flower, the true oxlip; and species of wild orchid, spurge laurel, ramson (wild garlic), currant and spindle, bluebells, bugles and anemones that make the sixteen-acre wood a delight in springtime, where the ash and oak on our boulder clay provide singing rostrums for warblers and tits.

Two new Ashdonians entered the lounge; well-shod, trendy dressed, their accents were those of spokesmen of radio and TV; but I understood the language of the next entrant, Cyril Williams, grandson of the late undertaker and builder, Starchy.

'Glad ter see yer, Ced. Pity you worn't earlier, ole Wal Marsh the hurdle maker wor ninety yisterday. He'll be abed by now.' I sent Walter a message. Upset, I looked out of the window, to see a motor car at almost every cottage, but not a soul walking on Crown Hill. Blinds were drawn, as though for the passing of our old village. Identical flickerings of light and shade appeared on all the blinds at the same time. I looked to the stars, almost obscured by TV aerials, and thought of other things . . .

> Long since, in England's pleasant lands
> I used to see the farming-hands.
> I need but shut my eyes, and fast
> There comes a picture of the past,
> Of men and women, long since dead,
> Who battled with the earth for bread
> (A daily bread they might but taste)
> For Folly and his doll to waste.
>
> *Land workers* JOHN MASEFIELD (1878–1968)

Index of names and crafts

Index of names and crafts

Index of names and crafts